THE ART OF CRAFTING COCKTAILS

HANDBOOK FOR THE FUTURE MIXOLOGIST

by

Paolo Patitucci

Here, you will learn the art of mixology, cocktail preparation techniques, and the secrets to creating extraordinary beverages.

PREFACE

WELCOME TO YOUR JOURNEY TOWARDS MIXOLOGY MASTERY

This guide is your gateway to the captivating world of bartending and mixology. Within these pages, you will embark on a quest to explore the intricate craft of cocktail-making, transforming it into an art form where creativity and expertise converge.

EMBARKING ON THE MIXOLOGY ODYSSEY

Welcome to a world where libations transform into works of art, and the bartender evolves into a mixologist. This manual is your compass as we navigate the exciting journey of becoming a true master of the craft. To reach this pinnacle, it requires not only time but unwavering passion and dedication.

This voyage promises to shape you into an exceptional mixologist, one who can transform each glass into a masterpiece, entertaining and surprising guests like no other.

ICHI-GO ICHI-E PHILOSOPHY

WHERE EVERY DRINK IS A MASTERPIECE, AND EVERY MOMENT IS A TREASURE TO BE CHERISHED

Throughout my career in the luxury hotel and restaurant

industry, spanning over two decades and taking me to various countries including Italy, the UK, Vietnam, Australia, and Turks and Caicos, I have accumulated invaluable experience and knowledge in the art of mixology.

In the realm of mixology and cocktail culture, I wholeheartedly embrace the Japanese philosophy of **Ichi-Go Ichi-E**.

This concept reminds me that each moment is unique and fleeting, inspiring me to craft unforgettable experiences through my expertise.

My approach is straightforward yet profound: I consider mixology an art form. I am not merely a creator of drinks; I aspire to be a conductor of moments. Each cocktail I craft is intended to be a masterpiece, meticulously created with mindfulness and unwavering attention to detail. I encourage my patrons to fully immerse themselves in the present.

Embracing Ichi-Go Ichi-E involves savoring the distinctive flavors, aromas, and textures of each cocktail. **It's essential to recognize that this moment, this drink, is one-of-a-kind and should be cherished.**

Our mission as mixologists is crystal clear: to elevate mixology to an art form and provide unforgettable experiences. We aim to foster a deeper connection between ourselves and the craft of cocktail-making, in turn creating enduring memories for our clientele.

For aspiring mixologists who have perused this book, I ask you not only to absorb the philosophy and approach I've shared but to engrain it into your very being.

ADOPT THE ICHI-GO ICHI-E PHILOSOPHY IN YOUR JOURNEY, JUST AS I HAVE.

Experiment, travel, visit bars, and connect with bartenders and mixologists from around the world. Each moment and interaction can offer unique insights and inspiration, thus making your mixology journey genuinely exceptional.

INTRODUCTION

THE ELEMENTS THAT MAKE THE PERFECT COCKTAIL

In mixology, crafting the perfect cocktail is an intricate art, influenced by factors like ingredients, techniques, glassware, and garnishes. However, the key factor is the bartender. They shape the cocktail's excellence from start to finish.

1. CHOOSING THE INGREDIENTS

An extraordinary cocktail begins with the selection of the finest ingredients. Liquors and spirits form the foundation of every creation. Knowing the different categories of spirits, such as bourbon, gin, rum, and vodka, is essential.

Each category brings with it a unique range of flavors and flavor profiles, offering endless opportunities to create surprising combinations. Choosing the right product is the first step toward perfection.

An experienced mixologist knows the various brands, the flavor differences among them, and can recommend the best product for each cocktail. Furthermore, they can tell the story behind the liquor, adding a touch of culture and history to the customer's experience.

2. METHOD AND TECHNIQUE OF PREPARATION

Preparing a cocktail requires more than simply mixing the ingredients. Preparation techniques, such as shaking, building, diluting, or muddling, are essential tools for creating a perfect balance.

Time and dilution influence the texture and flavor of the cocktail. An experienced mixologist knows the techniques and knows when and how to apply them to achieve the desired result.

Each technique has an impact on the consistency and appearance of the cocktail, as well as its flavor. Choosing the right technique is an integral part of the mixologist's creativity.

3. GLASS SELECTION AND PRESENTATION

The choice of glass plays a crucial role in the presentation of the cocktail. Each type of glass offers a unique sensation and can influence the tactile perception of the experience.

Glass choice goes beyond aesthetic appearance; it is an integral part of the experience that the mixologist wants to provide to their customers. The presentation of the cocktail, including the choice of glass, garnish, and final color, is an art in itself and adds a touch of magic to the drink's experience. Furthermore, it is important to follow a presentation standard: cocktails with clear spirits, such as Vodka Soda or Gin and Tonic, are traditionally served in tall glasses to maintain effervescence and freshness.

On the other hand, cocktails with dark spirits, such as Rum and Cola or Whiskey Ginger Ale, are often served in low glasses to emphasize the complex flavors of aged liquors. Be creative in your glass selection and transform cocktail service into an extraordinary experience.

4. BALANCING THE INGREDIENTS

An expert mixologist knows that balancing the ingredients is the essence of an exceptional cocktail. The 2:1:1 rule, which establishes the ratio between the main spirit, flavored liquor, and aromatic component, is a fundamental starting point.

However, the ability to adapt this balance to suit the customer's taste is what sets a true professional apart. They know when to follow traditional rules and when to challenge them to create a unique drink.

They understand not only the proportions but also the importance of using fresh, high-quality ingredients. The skill to skill fully balance elements of sweetness, acidity, bitterness, and alcohol is the secret to captivating the customer's palate.

5. THE BARTENDER: THE KEY TO SUCCESS

Every element mentioned so far is influenced and controlled by a single individual: the bartender. The mixologist is the conductor of this symphony of flavors and techniques.

Their knowledge, creativity, skill, and attention to detail are what make the creation of extraordinary cocktails possible. The mixologist is the key to a drink's success and the guarantor of the customer's experience. The bartender is not just a cocktail creator but also a storyteller who can enrich the customer's experience with anecdotes about the origins of the cocktail and curious facts about various ingredients. Their confidence and expertise influence the customer's perception and create a more engaging drinking experience.

6. ICE QUALITY

Often overlooked, ice is a fundamental element for the perfect cocktail. The purity of ice, its size, and shape influence dilution and cooling of the drink. Some cocktails require clear, crystalline ice, while others can benefit from hand-carved ice cubes or ice spheres. The mixologist knows which type of ice suits each creation best and understands its impact on the final result. They understand the importance of using fresh and high-quality ice to avoid compromising the cocktail's flavor. Additionally, the mixologist is aware that ice is a visual and tactile element of the drink, which can influence the overall customer experience.

7. WELL-ORGANIZED MIXOLOGY STATION

In the pursuit of creating the perfect cocktail, one often under-appreciated aspect is the organization of your mixology station.

A well-organized station not only enhances your efficiency but also elevates your craft to a professional level. In the pages that follow, you will learn how to make the most of every inch of your workspace, ensuring minimal movement and maximum ease in accessing your ingredients.

8. KNOWLEDGE OF CLASSIC AND MODERN COCKTAILS

In the world of mixology, having a deep understanding of classic and modern cocktail recipes is essential. A skilled mixologist should be well-versed in the history, ingredients, and preparation methods of both time-honored classics and contemporary creations. This knowledge allows the mixologist to provide customers with a wide array of options and recommendations.

Furthermore, staying updated on modern cocktail trends and new recipes allows the mixologist to offer innovative and exciting options to patrons who are looking for something fresh and unique. The ability to create, modify, and perfect these recipes is a testament to a mixologist's skill and adaptability, ultimately enriching the customer's experience by catering to their individual preferences.

In this space dedicated to mixology, we will explore every aspect of this fascinating art, from ingredient selection to preparation techniques, from presentation to storytelling about the stories behind each cocktail. The mixologist is much more than a mere bartender: they are an artist, an alchemist, and a host.

CHAPTER 1
LIQUORS AND SPIRITS

In the realm of mixology, mastering the art of creating exceptional cocktails requires a deep understanding of the diverse world of spirits and liqueurs. These two categories of alcoholic beverages form the backbone of mixology, and knowing their unique characteristics is paramount to crafting memorable drinks.

SPIRITS

Also known as distillates or hard liquors, are pure and undiluted alcoholic beverages derived through the process of distillation.

They are the unadulterated essence of a particular grain, fruit, or botanical, and each spirit has its own distinct flavor profile.

Spirits serve as the foundation for countless classic and contemporary cocktails, and their attributes can significantly influence the taste of a drink. Mixologists often refer to spirits in terms of their proof, which indicates their alcohol content. Understanding the proof of a spirit helps a mixologist gauge the intensity and balance of a cocktail.

LIQUEURS

They, are a delightful realm of flavored and often sweetened spirits.

Liqueurs are created by infusing various ingredients, including herbs, fruits, nuts, or spices, into a base spirit. Liqueurs bring depth, complexity, and a touch of sweetness to cocktails, making them an essential tool in a mixologist's arsenal.

The selection of liqueurs also involves considerations of sweetness and viscosity, as these factors greatly affect the overall mouthfeel and consistency of a drink.

In this chapter, we will delve into the world of spirits and liqueurs, exploring their different types, characteristics, and suggested pairings.

Whether you're a seasoned mixologist or just beginning your journey, this knowledge will enrich your craft and help you create cocktails that leave a lasting impression.

WHISKEY

Whiskey is a distilled alcoholic beverage made from grains such as barley, rye, corn, or wheat. There are various types of whiskey, each with a unique flavor profile.

WHISKEY BOURBON

Characteristics

Bourbon is American whiskey primarily produced in the United States, with Kentucky being its most well-known place of origin. Bourbon is characterized by rich flavors of vanilla, caramel, and sweetness derived from aging in charred oak barrels. It's a key ingredient in cocktails like the classic Old Fashioned and Whiskey Sour.

Pairings

Bourbon pairs perfectly with sweet ingredients like honey, maple syrup, dehydrated pears and apples, banana, coconut, cinnamon and chocolate, creating balanced and enveloping cocktails.

WHISKEY RYE

Characteristics

Rye whiskey is known for its distinctive spicy and earthy flavor. It's often used in cocktails to add a touch of complexity. Rye whiskey is produced in the United States and Canada. It works well in cocktails like the Manhattan and Old Fashioned.

Pairings

Rye is an ideal choice for cocktails with caramel, maple syrup, spicy and citrus notes, offering a pleasant complexity.

SCOTCH WHISKEY

Characteristics

Scotch whisky comes from Scotland and is divided into various categories, including single malt and blended Scotch. Scotch is famous for its smoky, peaty, and fruity notes. It's the main ingredient in cocktails like the Rob Roy and Blood and Sand.

Pairings

Experiment with Scottish whisky in smoky cocktails or in combinations with fruit to create unique sensory experiences.

JAPANESE WHISKY

Characteristics

Japanese whisky has gained renown for its elegance and sophistication. It often features fruity, floral, and slightly spicy notes. Japanese whisky is used in many cocktails especially for High-Balls in Japan and can be sipped neat to appreciate its sublime flavors.

Pairings

Explore the art of the Japanese Highball, serving Japanese whisky with sparkling water and a twist of citrus for a refreshing and harmonious drink

GIN

Gin is a clear spirit flavored primarily with botanicals, including juniper berries. It's known for its versatility and ability to create a wide range of cocktails. The flavors of gin can vary depending on the botanicals used:

LONDON DRY GIN

Characteristics

This style is dry, crisp, and juniper-forward. It's the standard choice for classic gin cocktails like the Gin Martini and Negroni.

Pairings

Enhance the herbal and citrus notes of London Dry Gin by choosing quality tonic water and garnishing with fresh citrus peels and botanicals.

PLYMOUTH GIN

Characteristics

Plymouth Gin is a softer and more aromatic gin, known for its earthy, sweet, and citrus notes. It's a great choice for cocktails like the Clover Club and White Lady.

Pairings

The softness of Plymouth Gin pairs wonderfully with herbal and citrus flavors in cocktails, such as thyme or orange peel garnishes.

NEW WESTERN DRY GIN

Characteristics

This style of gin focuses on a wider range of botanicals, allowing for more creativity in cocktails. Hendrick's is a popular example, known for its cucumber and rose petal notes. It can be used in creative concoctions like the Cucumber Collins.

Pairings

Embrace the unique botanicals in New Western Dry Gins and experiment with complementary ingredients such as cucumber, elderflower, or rose water serving your Gin and Tonic in a balloon glass.

RUM

Rum is a distilled spirit made from sugarcane or molasses. It varies in flavor, from light and crisp to dark and rich. There are various types of rum, such as white, gold, dark, and spiced

WHITE RUM

Characteristics

White rum is light and slightly sweet, often used in tropical cocktails like the Daiquiri and Mojito.

Pairings

Utilize white rum's neutrality to create refreshing, fruit-forward cocktails with flavors like lime, coconut, and mint.

GOLD RUM

Characteristics

Gold rum is aged for a short period, gaining a touch of caramel and vanilla notes. It's suitable for cocktails like the Mai Tai and Rum Punch.

Pairings

Experiment with gold rum's subtle complexity by incorporating tropical fruits like pineapple and passion fruit for a balanced, exotic taste.

DARK RUM

Characteristics

Dark rum is aged for an extended period, resulting in rich, molasses, and oak notes. It's a key component in drinks like the Dark 'n' Stormy and Zombie.

Pairings

Complement the depth of dark rum with bold spices and tropical ingredients, such as ginger beer or allspice dram.

SPICED RUM

Characteristics

Spiced rum features a blend of spices, offering a warm and aromatic profile. It's often used in cocktails like the Spiced Rum Sour and Painkiller.

Pairings

Highlight the spiced notes in cocktails by incorporating ingredients like cinnamon, cloves, or fresh nutmeg.

AGRICULTURAL RUM

Characteristics

Agricultural rum is made from fresh sugarcane juice rather than molasses. This gives agricultural rum a vegetal, grassy, and slightly citrusy flavor.

Pairings

To accentuate the agricultural character of rum, use fresh ingredients like lime and cane syrup for a tropical twist.

VODKA

Vodka is a versatile and neutral distilled spirit known for its clean and crisp flavor profile. It is a key ingredient in many classic cocktails and offers a blank canvas for mixologists to create a wide range of drinks.

WHEAT VODKA

Characteristics

Wheat vodka is made from wheat grains, offering a slightly creamy and sweet undertone. It's known for its smooth and pure flavor.

Pairings

Wheat vodka's subtle sweetness makes it an excellent choice for cocktails with citrus and herbal elements, such as the Lemon Drop Martini or the Moscow Mule.

POTATO VODKA

Characteristics

Potato vodka is distilled from potatoes, giving it a distinct creaminess and earthiness. It's considered to have a richer mouthfeel.

Pairings

Potato vodka complements cocktails with creamy or savory elements. Try it in drinks like the Dirty Martini or the Bloody Mary for added depth.

RYE VODKA

Characteristics

Rye vodka is crafted from rye grains, resulting in a slightly spicier and bolder flavor compared to other varieties.

Pairings

Rye vodka pairs well with cocktails that feature bold and spicy flavors, such as the Black Russian or the Moscow Mule.

CORN VODKA

Characteristics

Corn vodka is made from corn grains, offering a naturally sweeter and smoother taste.

Pairings

Corn vodka works exceptionally well in cocktails with fruity and sweet elements. Consider using it for your Vodka Martini, the resultsPIt's a clean and crisp cocktail with a subtle sweetness from the corn vodka.

E. GRAPE VODKA

Characteristics

Grape vodka, often referred to as "grappa," is distilled from grapes. It boasts a unique fruitiness and floral aroma.

Pairings

Grape vodka enhances cocktails with its fruity character. Try it in drinks like the Grape Cosmo or the Grape Sour for a delightful twist.

TEQUILA AND MEZCAL

In the captivating world of mixology, two Mexican spirits, Tequila and Mezcal, stand as distinctive expressions of culture, craftsmanship, and flavor. These agave-based spirits are essential to a mixologist's repertoire, each with its unique characteristics and a rich history that adds depth and flavor to the world of cocktails.

TEQUILA

DISTILLATION

Tequila is typically distilled in pot stills or column stills, known as "Alambiques." The distillation process can be done twice or more to achieve the desired purity and flavor profile. High-quality tequilas are usually distilled two or three times, resulting in a smoother and purer spirit.

FLAVOR NOTES

- **Blanco (Silver):** Blanco tequila offers a clean and crisp taste with a prominent agave flavor, sometimes featuring herbal and earthy notes. It is typically unaged or aged for a very short period, often less than two months.
- **Reposado (Rested):** The aging process in oak barrels adds subtle hints of vanilla and caramel to the agave character, creating a more complex flavor profile. Reposado tequila is aged in oak barrels for a minimum of two months and up to one year.
- **Añejo (Aged):** Añejo tequila has a rich and complex character with pronounced caramel and oak flavors, similar to aged spirits like whiskey. It is aged in oak barrels for at least one year and up to three years.
- **Extra Añejo (Ultra-Aged):** Extra Añejo tequila has an extremely smooth and sophisticated profile, often reminiscent of well-aged spirits like cognac or Scotch whisky. It is aged for a minimum of three years.

USAGE

- **Blanco** tequila is excellent for cocktails where the agave flavor should shine through, such as Margaritas and Palomas.
- **Reposado** tequila can add depth to cocktails that require a balance between agave notes and subtle wood or vanilla hints.
- **Añejo and Extra Añejo** tequilas are typically sipped neat to appreciate their rich and complex character, but they can also be used in high-end cocktails that benefit from their mature flavor profile.

PAIRINGS

Pairing Tequila with complementary ingredients can enhance your cocktails. Here are some suggested pairings for Tequila:

- **Blanco Tequila:** Combines beautifully with citrus fruits such as lime and orange, as well as sweeteners like agave nectar or honey. Spices like cinnamon and chili can add depth and complexity to cocktails made with Blanco Tequila.
- **Reposado Tequila:** Works well with flavors like vanilla and caramel, making it a good match for cocktails featuring cinnamon or other warm spices. It also complements citrus fruits and tropical flavors like pineapple.
- **Añejo** Tequila: Pairs wonderfully with rich, dark flavors such as dark chocolate, coffee, or espresso. It can also be a great base for cocktails with aged cheeses and nutty undertones.

MEZCAL

DISTILLATION

Mezcal traditionally undergoes distillation in clay pots or wooden barrels. This traditional method, known as "Palenque," contributes to mezcal's smoky and earthy qualities. The art of making mezcal often involves variations in distillation techniques and materials, leading to diverse flavor profiles among different brands and types.

FLAVOR NOTES

- **Joven (Young or Silver):** Joven mezcal, being unaged, typically showcases pure agave notes with a prominent smokiness and earthiness. Some joven mezcals may have fruity undertones.
- **Reposado (Rested):** Aging in barrels adds milder smokiness and subtle wood notes to reposado mezcal, creating a balanced profile with smokiness and other flavors. Reposado mezcal is aged in barrels for a minimum of two months.
- **Añejo (Aged):** Añejo mezcal is known for its refined and complex character, often featuring smoky, woody, and fruity elements. It can be as diverse as aged tequila or whisky. Añejo mezcal is aged in barrels for at least one year and up to three years.

USAGE

- **Joven** mezcal's distinctive smokiness and earthiness make it perfect for cocktails that aim to highlight these qualities, such as the Mezcal Margarita or Oaxaca Old Fashioned.
- **Reposado** mezcal can offer a balanced smoky-sweet profile that pairs well with citrus, honey, or cinnamon, creating versatile cocktails.
- **Añejo** mezcal's complex notes make it an excellent choice for crafting cocktails with rich and deep flavors, such as those incorporating aged cheeses, dark chocolate, or espresso.

PAIRINGS

Pairing Tequila and Mezcal with complementary ingredients is an art that can elevate your cocktails to new heights. Here are some suggested pairings:

- **Tequila,** especially Reposado and Añejo, pairs wonderfully with citrus fruits like lime and orange, as well as sweeteners such as agave nectar or honey. Spices like cinnamon and chili add depth and complexity to tequila-based cocktails.
- **Mezcal's** smokiness makes it an ideal match for ingredients like grilled pineapple, chocolate bitters, or herbs like rosemary and thyme. The combination of smoky mezcal with spicy chili can create a delightful and intriguing flavor profile.

TEQUILA
MEZCAL
Various species of Agave
Should be 100% agave
Origins span across all nine Mexican states
Smoky and caramelized flavor
Only Blue Agave
Required to have 51% agave
Jalisco is home to about 99% of all tequila
Aroma and flavour is neutral

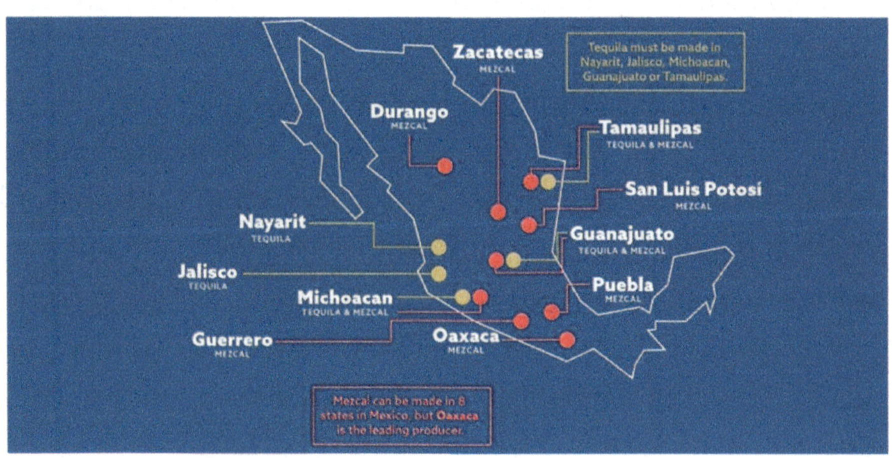
Zacatecas
MEZCAL
Tequila must be made in Nayarit, Jalisco, Michoacan, Guanajuato or Tamaulipas.
Durango
MEZCAL
Tamaulipas
TEQUILA & MEZCAL
San Luis Potosí
MEZCAL
Nayarit
TEQUILA
Guanajuato
TEQUILA & MEZCAL
Jalisco
TEQUILA
Puebla
MEZCAL
Michoacan
TEQUILA & MEZCAL
Guerrero
MEZCAL
Oaxaca
MEZCAL
Mezcal can be made in 8 states in Mexico, but Oaxaca is the leading producer.

LIQUORS AND CORDIALS

Liqueurs and cordials are essential for creating cocktails with depth and complexity. These flavored spirits can add sweetness, bitterness, or a variety of unique flavors to your drinks. Here are some key liqueurs and cordials that every mixologist should have in their toolkit

TRIPLE SEC

Characteristics

Triple sec is a sweet orange liqueur, often used to add citrusy sweetness to cocktails like the Margarita and Whiskey Sour..

Pairings

Try different brands of triple sec to find one that best complements your cocktail's flavor profile.

COINTREAU

Characteristics

Cointreau is a premium triple sec with a clear, crisp orange flavor. It's a favorite choice for classic cocktails.

Pairings

Cointreau's balanced sweetness and bright citrus notes make it ideal for enhancing the aroma and flavor of cocktails.

CURAÇAO

Characteristics

Curaçao is a citrus-flavored liqueur, often used to add color and a citrusy twist to cocktails. It comes in various colors, including blue, orange, and clear.

Pairings

Experiment with different Curaçao colors to match the aesthetic and flavor of your cocktails.

GRAND MARNIER

Characteristics

Grand Marnier is a luxurious orange liqueur made from Cognac and exotic oranges. It adds complexity and depth to cocktails, such as the Margarita and Cosmopolitan.

Pairings

Incorporate Grand Marnier to create more refined and intricate cocktails with a hint of Cognac's elegance.

CHAMBORD

Characteristics

Chambord is a black raspberry liqueur with a rich, fruity flavor. It's perfect for adding a touch of berry sweetness to cocktails like the French Martini and Chambord Sour.

Pairings

Chambord's vibrant fruitiness complements other berry-based ingredients, making it an excellent choice for berry-infused cocktails.

AMARETTO

Characteristics

Amaretto is a sweet almond-flavored liqueur. It's used in cocktails like the Amaretto Sour and Godfather.

Pairings

Enhance the nutty character of amaretto by pairing it with other nut-flavored ingredients or warm spices like cinnamon.

COFFEE LIQUEUR

Characteristics

Coffee liqueur, such as Kahlúa, adds rich coffee flavor and sweetness to cocktails like the White Russian and Espresso Martini.

Pairings

Combine coffee liqueur with other complementary flavors like cream or chocolate for decadent coffee-based cocktails.

IRISH CREAM LIQUEUR

Characteristics

Irish cream liqueur, like Baileys, infuses cocktails with a creamy, sweet, and slightly chocolatey profile. It's a delightful addition to drinks like the Mudslide and B-52.

Pairings

Irish cream liqueur can be used in both hot and cold drinks, making it a versatile ingredient for various occasions.

FRANGELICO

Characteristics

Frangelico is a hazelnut liqueur with a distinct nutty flavor. It's used in cocktails like the Nutty Irishman and Frangelico Sour.

Pairings

Combine Frangelico with other nut liqueurs or flavors like chocolate and vanilla for indulgent, nutty cocktails.

GALLIANO

Characteristics

Galliano is a bright yellow herbal liqueur with vanilla and anise notes. It's used in cocktails like the Harvey Wallbanger and Golden Cadillac.

Pairings

Galliano's unique flavors are showcased in retro cocktails, so experiment with classic recipes to appreciate its charm.

MELON LIQUEUR

Characteristics

Melon liqueur, like Midori, has a vibrant melon flavor that's perfect for cocktails like the Midori Sour and Melon Ball.

Pairings

Highlight the fresh and fruity notes of melon liqueur by pairing it with other vibrant fruit juices and spirits.

CRÈME DE CACAO

Characteristics

Crème de Cacao is a sweet chocolate-flavored liqueur, often used in cocktails like the Chocolate Martini.

Pairings

Combine crème de Cacao with various cream liqueurs and spirits for a delightful range of chocolate-infused drinks.

CRÈME DE MENTHE

Characteristics

Crème de Menthe is a mint-flavored liqueur used to add a refreshing, minty twist to cocktails like the Grasshopper and Stinger.

Pairings

Use crème de Menthe to create cooling and minty cocktails by incorporating other minty ingredients or chocolates.

MARASCHINO LIQUEUR

Characteristics

Maraschino liqueur is made from sour marasca cherries, adding a unique sweet and slightly bitter flavor to cocktails like the Aviation and Last Word.

Pairings

Maraschino liqueur provides a distinctive cherry flavor, so explore classic cocktails that highlight its fruity character.

BITTERS AND APERITIVES

Bitters and Cordials are indispensable for crafting cocktails with depth and complexity. These infused or flavored spirits introduce a diverse range of tastes, from sweet and bitter to unique and exotic.

CAMPARI

Characteristics

Campari is a bright red Italian bitter liqueur, known for its complex herbal and citrus notes. It's a crucial ingredient in cocktails like the Negroni and Americano.

Pairings

Balance Campari's bitterness with sweet or herbal elements to create well-rounded cocktails.

APEROL

Characteristics

Aperol is a milder Italian bitter liqueur with pronounced orange and herbal flavors. It's the star of the Aperol Spritz and Aperol Sour.

Pairings

Aperol's approachable bitterness makes it perfect for light, refreshing cocktails with a bitter-sweet profile.

BENEDICTINE

Characteristics

Benedictine is a herbal liqueur with a complex flavor profile, featuring honey, citrus, and various spices. It's used in cocktails like the Bobby Burns and Vieux Carré.

Pairings

Explore Benedictine's complexity by incorporating it into cocktails with a range of herbal and aromatic ingredients.

CHARTREUSE

Characteristics

Chartreuse is a French herbal liqueur with variations in green and yellow. Its flavor is bold, herbal, and slightly sweet, making it an essential element in cocktails like the Last Word and Bijou.

Pairings

Chartreuse's bold flavors can dominate a cocktail, so use it sparingly and thoughtfully.

DRAMBUIE

Characteristics

Drambuie is a Scotch whisky liqueur with honey and herbal flavors. It adds warmth and complexity to cocktails like the Rusty Nail and Bobby Burns.

Pairings

Incorporate Drambuie into whisky-based cocktails to enhance their sweetness and complexity.

ABSINTHE

Characteristics

Absinthe is an anise-flavored spirit known for its intense herbal profile. It's used in classic cocktails like the Sazerac and Corpse Reviver.

Pairings

Absinthe is a powerful ingredient, so use it sparingly to impart anise and herbal notes to your drinks.

SAMBUCA

Characteristics

Sambuca is an anise-flavored liqueur often enjoyed as a digestive, but it's also used in cocktails like the Black Russian and Flaming Sambuca.

Pairings

When using Sambuca in cocktails, consider its anise flavor and pair it with ingredients that complement or contrast its licorice notes.

BRANDY AND COGNAC

Both brandy and cognac are important for mixologists because they offer rich, complex flavors that can add depth and sophistication to cocktails, making them essential components in crafting classic and contemporary drinks

BRANDY

Characteristics

Brandy can range from sweet and fruity to dry and rich. It's used in cocktails like the Sidecar and Brandy Alexander.

Pairings

Choose brandy based on the cocktail's profile, using sweeter brandies for dessert cocktails and drier ones for classics like the Sidecar.

COGNAC

Characteristics

Cognac is a specific type of brandy produced in the Cognac region of France. It's renowned for its elegance, complexity, and aging potential. Cognac is the star of cocktails like the French 75 and Sazerac.

Pairings

Savor the nuances of cognac by stirring it in classic cocktails to maintain its rich and complex character.

CHAPTER 2
ESSENTIAL BITTERS AND TINCTURE

Their origins can be traced back to the historical use of botanicals, herbs, spices, and roots for their therapeutic properties. In times gone by, these concentrated extracts played a crucial role in alleviating a myriad of ailments.

ESSENTIAL TINCTURES

Tinctures have undergone a fascinating transformation from ancient remedies to contemporary mixological marvels. Their rich history, infusion techniques, and modern applications combine to offer a wide spectrum of flavors, aromas, and depths to the world of cocktails. Subsequent chapters will delve deeper into the nuances of these concentrated extracts, exploring their characteristics, flavor profiles, and the artistry of mixologists, providing a comprehensive guide to the universe of bitters and tinctures.

ROOT TINCTURES: HISTORY, APPLICATION

Historical Uses: Root tinctures, like those made from angelica or ginseng, were popular for their energy-boosting and immune-strengthening properties. These extracts were meticulously created through the infusion of dried roots in alcohol, promising better health to those who consumed them.

Infusion Techniques: The art of infusing roots in alcohol, a process that involves time and precision, led to the creation of aromatic and potent root tinctures. Each root required a unique approach to capture its essence.

Modern Application: In the modern mixologist's toolkit, root tinctures are employed to introduce complexity and earthy undertones to cocktails. They offer depth and a hint of history, creating a distinctive drinking experience.

HERBAL TINCTURES

Historical Significance: Herbal tinctures, featuring ingredients like chamomile and lavender, were historically used to calm nerves, reduce anxiety, and induce restful sleep. They were prepared through the infusion of aromatic herbs in alcohol, promoting overall well-being.

Infusion Mastery: The process of infusing herbs in alcohol is an art in itself, requiring precision to capture the soothing properties of herbs accurately.

Contemporary Application: In modern mixology, herbal tinctures are harnessed to introduce tranquility and a natural aroma to cocktails, resulting in beverages that go beyond mere taste.

SPICED TINCTURES

Traditional Remedies: Spiced tinctures, infused with spices like cinnamon, cloves, and cardamom, were traditionally used to alleviate digestive discomfort and enhance digestion. They were known for their fragrant and soothing qualities.

Spice Infusion: Infusing spices in alcohol necessitates an understanding of the unique characteristics of each spice. The process was delicate but rewarding, resulting in extracts filled with aromatic warmth.

Modern Mixology: In today's mixology scene, spiced tinctures bring fragrant and digestive qualities to cocktails, enriching them with an array of flavors and comforting aromatics.

CRAFTING YOUR OWN TINCTURES

Essential Ingredients: To craft unique tinctures, it's crucial to understand the diverse ingredients available, each with its distinct characteristics and flavor profiles.

Infusion Methods: Various methods and techniques exist for creating bespoke tinctures. Each method influences the final product's taste and aroma.

Mixologist's Touch: Seasoned mixologists offer insights into using tinctures effectively. They share their expertise on adding depth and character to cocktails, turning ordinary drinks into extraordinary experiences.

ESSENTIAL BITTERS

In the world of mixology, bitters are like the artist's palette, allowing you to paint your cocktails with a broad spectrum of flavors. These concentrated flavoring agents can transform the profile of a cocktail with just a few drops. In this chapter, we'll explore the diverse world of essential bitters and tinctures, discussing their flavors, compositions, usage, pairings, and offering mixologist tips on how to harness their potential in crafting exceptional drinks.

ANGOSTURA BITTERS: HARMONY OF HERBS, SPICES, AND CITRUS

Flavor: Angostura bitters are known for their harmonious blend of herbs, spices, and citrus notes.

Composition: The exact recipe is a well-guarded secret, but it includes a variety of botanicals and spices.

Usage: Angostura bitters can be used to balance sweetness in cocktails and enhance aromatic complexity.

Pairings: They complement classics like the Old Fashioned and Manhattan.

PEYCHAUD'S BITTERS: NEW ORLEANS ESSENCE

Flavor: Peychaud's bitters have a distinct licorice and anise profile with a hint of floral notes.

Composition: The exact recipe remains a mystery, but it's known for its anise and floral components.

Usage: Incorporate Peychaud's bitters to create cocktails with a touch of New Orleans flair and complexity.

Pairings: Essential for the Sazerac cocktail and other New Orleans classics.

Mixologist's Tip: Harness the essence of New Orleans by adding Peychaud's bitters to your creations.

ORANGE BITTERS: CITRUS ZEST IN A BOTTLE

Flavor: Orange bitters provide a bright and zesty citrus element.

Composition: Ingredients vary, but orange peels and spices play a central role.

Usage: Experiment with orange bitters to enhance the aroma and flavor of cocktails with citrus notes.

Pairings: Ideal for classics like the Martini and Pegu Club.

Mixologist's Tip: Elevate your Martini cocktails with a burst of citrus using orange bitters.

AROMATIC BITTERS: SPICE AND HERB SYMPHONY

Flavor: Aromatic bitters offer a balance of spices and herbs, adding complexity to cocktails.

Composition: Ingredients include a blend of spices, herbs, and botanicals.

Usage: Use aromatic bitters to introduce subtle complexity and depth to various cocktails.

Pairings: Versatile in classics like the Whiskey Sour and Champagne Cocktail.

Mixologist's Tip: Create a symphony of flavors in your Old Fashioned with aromatic bitters.

CHOCOLATE BITTERS: DECADENT COCOA FLAVORS

Flavor: Chocolate bitters add rich, cocoa notes to cocktails, making them dessert-inspired.

Composition: Ingredients may include cocoa, spices, and botanicals.

Usage: Incorporate chocolate bitters to enhance the chocolate profile in drinks.

Pairings: Perfect for cocktails like the Chocolate Old Fashioned and Chocolate Martini.

Mixologist's Tip: Create decadent Spiced Rum Old-fashioned with a touch of cocoa using chocolate bitters.

MINT BITTERS: MENTHOL FRESHNESS

Flavor: Mint bitters bring a refreshing minty twist to cocktails.

Composition: Ingredients typically include mint leaves and other botanicals.

Usage: Utilize mint bitters to create cooling and herbaceous cocktails with a minty finish.

Pairings: They work well in drinks like the Mint Julep and Whiskey Smash.

Mixologist's Tip: Give your whiskey sour s a minty burst of freshness with mint bitters.

CELERY BITTERS: UNCONVENTIONAL VEGETAL NOTES

Flavor: Celery bitters offer a unique vegetal note, often used in savory cocktails.

Composition: Ingredients often include celery, herbs, and spices.

Usage: Experiment with celery bitters to introduce savory and herbal elements into cocktails.

Pairings: Commonly used in drinks like the Bloody Mary and Celery Sour.

Mixologist's Tip: Add a touch of the garden to your Gin Martini with celery bitters

CARDAMOM BITTERS: WARM SPICE AND CITRUS

Flavor: Cardamom bitters provide warm, spicy, and citrusy notes to cocktails.

Composition: Ingredients include cardamom pods, spices, and botanicals.

Usage: Enhance the aromatic complexity of cocktails with cardamom bitters, adding an exotic twist.

Pairings: Suitable for cocktails like the Cardamom Sour and Winter Solstice.

Mixologist's Tip: Spice up your G&T with the warm embrace of cardamom bitters.

CHERRY BITTERS: FRUITY AND SWEET DELIGHT

Flavor: Cherry bitters have a sweet and fruity flavor that enhances various cocktails.

Composition: Ingredients typically include cherries, spices, and botanicals.

Usage: Combine cherry bitters with various spirits and fruit flavors to create cherry-infused cocktails.

Pairings: Perfect for drinks like the Cherry Old Fashioned and Cherry Collins.

Mixologist's Tip: Infuse your Manhattan with the delightful sweetness of cherry bitters.

GRAPEFRUIT BITTERS: CITRUS PUNCH IN A BOTTLE

Flavor: Grapefruit bitters bring a zesty and citrusy touch to cocktails.

Composition: Ingredients often feature grapefruit zest and spices.

Usage: Enhance the grapefruit notes in cocktails or add a refreshing twist by using grapefruit bitters.

Pairings: Suitable for drinks like the Grapefruit Negroni and Paloma.

Mixologist's Tip: Add a punch of citrus to your Negroni with the vibrant grapefruit bitters.

LAVENDER BITTERS: FRAGRANT AND FLORAL

Flavor: Lavender bitters have a floral and herbaceous profile, ideal for elegant cocktails.

Composition: Lavender blossoms and botanicals contribute to the flavor.

Usage: Infuse cocktails with the soothing and aromatic notes of lavender bitters, creating fragrant drinks.

Pairings: Ideal for cocktails like the Lavender Lemonade and Lavender Martini.

Mixologist's Tip: Elevate your Vodka Martini with the delicate aroma of lavender bitters.

SMOKE BITTERS: ADDING FIRE TO YOUR COCKTAILS

Flavor: Smoke bitters add smoky and spicy elements to cocktails, creating a bold profile.

Composition: Ingredients may include smoky chili and spices.

Usage: Experiment with smoke bitters to create cocktails with a smoky and fiery kick.

Pairings: Ideal for drinks like the Smoky Margarita and Spicy Blackberry Smash.

Mixologist's Tip: Ignite the flavor of Sazerac with the fire of smoke bitters.

BARREL-AGED BITTERS: AGED COMPLEXITY

Flavor: Barrel-aged bitters offer a rich and woody character with vanilla and spice notes.

Composition: Aging in barrels imparts depth to the flavor profile.

Usage: Enhance the depth of cocktails by incorporating barrel-aged bitters.

Pairings: Commonly used in drinks like the Barrel-Aged Vieux Carré and Barrel-Aged Manhattan.

Mixologist's Tip: Age your Old Fashioned with the richness of barrel-aged bitters.

CHAPTER 3
MASTERING INGREDIENT SELECTION

In the world of mixology, ingredient selection is a finely-honed craft. Beyond the basics, it's an art form that distinguishes the extraordinary from the mundane. This chapter is your gateway to advanced insights on selecting ingredients that will elevate your cocktails to new heights.

EXPLORING FLAVOURFUL DEPTHS WITH KEY COCKTAIL JUICES

PINEAPPLE JUICE: A TROPICAL ELEGANCE

Flavor Essence: Tropical sweetness and silky with a slightly thick texture. Learn to expertly employ it in cocktails like the Piña Colada, creating a velvety, enveloping experience.

Perfect Pairings: Pineapple juice harmonizes beautifully with rum and tequila, while coconut cream complements its tropical essence. Complement its fruity notes with dashes of passion fruit and mango.

ORANGE JUICE: CITRUSY ZEST AND SWEETNESS

Flavor Essence: Bright, citrusy, and slightly tangy charm, is known for its smooth, fluid texture. Discover how it adds juicy, refreshing aspects to cocktails like the Amaretto Sunrise.

Perfect Pairings: Tequila and orange liqueur find an ideal partner in orange juice, creating classics like the Margarita. Enhance its citrus profile with the zest of blood oranges or mandarins.

CRANBERRY JUICE: SWEETNESS AND ACIDITY

Flavor Essence: It offer a delightful blend of sweetness and acidity. Its slightly viscous texture brings complexity to cocktails, making it a go-to for drinks like the Cosmopolitan.

Perfect Pairings: Vodka and cranberry juice create the iconic Cosmopolitan. Add depth with a dash of Cointreau and fresh lime juice for a well-rounded experience.

GRAPEFRUIT JUICE: A ZESTY TWIST OF BITTERSWEET

Flavor Essence: Explore the zesty, bittersweet character of grapefruit juice, known for its tart and tangy flavor with a moderate consistency. Learn to use it in cocktails like the Greyhound to refresh and invigorate.

Perfect Pairings: Pair the zing of grapefruit juice with gin for a classic Greyhound. Add complexity with elderflower liqueur or a sprig of rosemary to elevate its aromatic aspects.

Balancing Sweetness: A Mixologist's Playground

HONEY: TRANSFORMING SWEETNESS INTO COMPLEXITY

Unlock the versatility of honey, going beyond sweetness to add complexity and depth. Delve into the nuances of acacia and chestnut honey and experience how they transform cocktails like the Gold Rush.

Liquid Partners: Bourbon and honey create a match made in heaven in the Gold Rush cocktail. Enhance honey's depth with a dash of aromatic bitters and a lemon twist.

HOMEMADE SYRUPS: CRAFTING CUSTOM FLAVOR LAYERS

Craft your own syrups for endless customization. Experiment with flavors like black pepper for a spicy kick or lavender for an unexpected floral aroma, adding unique layers to your cocktails.

Art of Mixology: Crafting your syrups allows for endless creativity. A black pepper syrup can add a spicy kick to a classic cocktail like the Whiskey Sour, and lavender syrup can provide an unexpected twist to a Gin Fizz.

MARMALADE: A TOUCH OF SWEETNESS AND FLAVOR

Witness how marmalade combines sweetness with a rich layer of flavor and texture in cocktails. Dive into the world of orange marmalade, infusing citrusy brightness and a touch of bitterness into classics like the Whiskey Sour.

Mingle with Spirits: The Whiskey Sour benefits from the complexity of marmalade, especially when paired with bourbon. Add a touch of orange bitters to enhance the citrus notes.

MAPLE SYRUP: EMBRACING NATURAL SWEETNESS

Explore the natural sweetness of maple syrup, enriched with hints of caramel and vanilla. Its viscosity and flavor make it ideal for classics like the Maple Old Fashioned, harmonizing beautifully with whiskey.

Sip and Savor: Maple syrup and bourbon make an excellent duo in the Maple Old Fashioned. Add depth with a dash of aromatic bitters and a flamed orange twist.

AGAVE NECTAR: MILD SWEETNESS WITH EARTHY NOTES

Learn how agave nectar, with its mild sweetness and earthy undertones, complements tequila-based cocktails. Discover its unique dimensions in drinks like the Margarita.

Tequila Companions: The Tommy's Margarita comes alive with agave nectar, enhancing the earthy aspects of tequila. A rim of chili salt or a splash of grapefruit juice can elevate the experience.

GRENADINE: VIBRANT COLOR AND SWEET-TART FLAVOR

Harness the vibrant red color and sweet-tart flavor of grenadine in your creations. Elevate classics like the Tequila Sunrise, creating visually appealing and delicious beverages.

Visual Delight: The Tequila Sunrise is a visual masterpiece with grenadine. Layer it with precision for that iconic sunrise effect. Experiment with different tequila expressions for diverse flavor profiles.

BALANCING ACIDITY AND ADDING COMPLEXITY

LEMON JUICE: THE ZEST OF FRESH ACIDITY

Discover the vibrant, tart, and fresh essence of lemon juice. Learn how it balances cocktails like the Whiskey Sour with its acidity.

Whiskey Companion: Lemon juice is the perfect counterbalance to the richness of bourbon in the Whiskey Sour. Fine-tune the experience with the choice of bourbon and a lemon twist.

LIME JUICE: THE INTENSITY OF ZESTY FRESHNESS

Explore the intensity of lime juice, with its distinct acidity and zesty freshness, a fundamental component in classics like the Margarita and Daiquiri.

Margarita Magic: Lime juice is the lifeblood of the Margarita. Combine it with tequila and orange liqueur for the perfect trifecta. Enhance the rim with chili salt or Tajin for a spicy kick.

CITRIC AND TARTARIC ACID: PRECISION IN ACIDITY

Dive into the world of precision by using citric and tartaric acids to regulate acidity without introducing additional flavors, a secret weapon for fine-tuning your cocktails.

The Art of Precision: Citric and tartaric acids are the mixologist's tools for precise acidity control. Experiment with acid solutions to perfect your cocktails, especially those that require a delicate touch.

ENHANCING FLAVOR WITH CREATIVITY

SMOKE INFUSER: TRANSFORMING WITH AROMATIC DEPTH

Witness how the smoke infuser transforms cocktails. Select aromatic woods like cherry or oak to add smoky depth to classics like the Boulevardier, creating unique and unforgettable sensory experiences.

Smoky Symphony: The Boulevardier takes on a new dimension with a touch of smokiness. Choose wood varieties to complement the cocktail's existing flavor profile, enhancing the overall experience.

FLAVORED FOAMS: AROMATIC SOPHISTICATION

Elevate your craft with flavored foams, whether it's coffee or mint. Offer a sophisticated, aromatic touch, creating olfactory experiences like an Irish Coffee with fresh coffee foam.

Foamy Elegance: Impress your patrons with a well-crafted foam. An Irish Coffee with fresh coffee foam adds a delightful olfactory element, setting it apart as a sensory delight.

WHIPPED CREAM: DECADENCE IN LIQUID FORM

Turn your cocktails into liquid desserts with a dollop of whipped cream. Create decadent experiences, like a Brandy Alexander topped with whipped cream and nutmeg.

Liquid Desserts: A Brandy Alexander reaches new heights with a dollop of whipped cream and a sprinkle of nutmeg. Elevate the presentation and provide a rich, indulgent finish to the cocktail.

CHAPTER 4
THE ART OF MIXING

In the world of mixology, crafting the perfect cocktail is more than just following a recipe; it's a delicate dance of techniques and tools that elevate ingredients into extraordinary libations. This chapter unveils the essential techniques every mixologist should master and the advanced knowledge that sets apart an exceptional cocktail maker.

THE HEART OF MIXOLOGY: THE ART OF MIXING

The art of mixing is the pivotal moment that turns a concoction of ingredients into a symphony of flavors. A skilled mixologist understands that beyond the recipe, it's the choice of technique and the right tools that ensure the perfect balance of taste and presentation. It's the difference between a mediocre drink and a masterpiece.

SHAKEN: THE VIGOROUS HARMONY

Technique

Shaking involves placing ingredients with ice in a cocktail shaker and giving it a vigorous shake. This rapid, high-energy method chills the cocktail swiftly and ensures even blending, making it ideal for drinks with fresh ingredients or fruit juices. Keep in mind that the duration of shaking influences dilution and cooling, so the choice is crucial. For example, a Martini requires well-chilled precision, which demands longer shaking, while a delicate Clover Club benefits from a gentler approach.

Mixology Tip: Shake with enthusiasm, but be mindful of the appropriate duration. Taste and adjust the dilution level to create the perfect cocktail.

BUILT: CRAFTING WITH PRECISION

Technique

Built cocktails are created by adding ingredients directly to the glass and then mixing with a long spoon or stirrer. This technique is favored for cocktails like the Moscow Mule or Aperol Spritz, where fresh ingredients require delicate handling. The advantage of this method is control; you can meticulously adjust the quantity of each ingredient to create the perfect balance. For example, in a Mojito, you can control the sweetness and acidity by varying the amount of lime juice or ginger syrup.

Mixology Tip: Take your time to layer ingredients precisely, making adjustments to suit your taste or your patrons' preferences.

STIRRED: THE ART OF CONTROLLED DILUTION

Technique

Stirred cocktails are created by gently stirring ingredients with ice in a glass, allowing the ice to melt and gradually dilute the cocktail. This technique is often used for cocktails made only with spirits like the Martini, where precise cooling and controlled dilution are vital. The level of dilution impacts the cocktail's strength and flavor profile. Sometimes, a slightly diluted Martini can be more inviting than a concentrated one.

Mixology Tip: Stir with patience, and taste along the way to ensure the ideal level of dilution and chill.

MUDDLED: GENTLY UNLEASHING FLAVORS

Technique

Muddling is the gentle art of mashing ingredients in the glass with a muddler. This releases essential oils and flavors from ingredients like mint leaves or fruit. It's a common practice in cocktails like the Mojito or Caipirinha. Muddling requires finesse to extract desired flavors without compromising the cocktail's texture. Over-muddling, as seen with mint leaves, can lead to bitterness in a Mojito.

Mixology Tip: Gently muddle ingredients to extract the desired flavors without overdoing it, ensuring a balanced and delightful drink.

HAWTHORN STRAINING TECHNIQUE: THE ESSENTIAL STRAIN

Technique

The Hawthorn straining technique, also known as "Hawthorn straining," is used to separate the cocktail from the ice or solid ingredients after shaking or stirring. The Hawthorn strainer, characterized by its coil-like spring and flat plate, is an indispensable tool. It's essential for cocktails like the Whiskey Sour or Margarita, ensuring that the chilled liquid flows smoothly into the serving glass while retaining the ice and preventing any unwanted solid materials.

Mixology Tip: Perfect your straining technique to avoid unwanted solids and ensure a seamless, visually appealing presentation.

LAYERED: CREATING VISUAL AND FLAVOR SPECTACLES

Technique

Layering is a captivating technique where different liquids are carefully poured into the glass to create distinct layers of color and flavor. Cocktails like the B-52 or Pousse-Café rely on this method to achieve visually appealing and unique presentations. Layering demands a gentle, controlled pour to avoid disturbing the layers and create a visually stunning result.

Mixology Tip: Master the art of pouring layers for cocktails that dazzle the eye as well as the palate.

BLENDED: A REFRESHING CONSISTENCY

Technique

Blending involves the art of mixing cocktail ingredients in a blender with ice to create a smooth, frothy texture. This technique is synonymous with tropical delights like the Piña Colada and Strawberry Daiquiri. The result is a delightful, slushy consistency that offers a refreshing and cooling experience, perfect for warm weather.

Mixology Tip: Achieve the perfect blend to create a luscious, chilled concoction that transports your patrons to a tropical paradise.

DRY SHAKE: CREATING CREAMY FROTH

Technique

The dry shake technique is a two-step process involving shaking cocktail ingredients without ice first, followed by a second shake with ice. This method is often used for cocktails containing egg whites, such as the Whiskey Sour, to create a frothy and creamy texture. The initial dry shake emulsifies the egg whites before chilling the drink with ice.

Mixology Tip: Dry shake with precision to achieve a velvety froth that adds a luxurious touch to cocktails.

FLAMED: A FIERY ELEGANCE

Technique

Flaming a cocktail briefly ignites a spirit on the surface of the drink to release aromatic oils and impart a subtle charred flavor. While this method is less common, it adds a unique sensory element to cocktails like the Sazerac or Blue Blazer. It should be executed with proper tools and caution due to open flames.

Mixology Tip: Approach flaming with care, and only attempt it if you're confident and have the right tools to create a mesmerizing sensory experience.

In addition to mastering these techniques, an experienced mixologist knows when to apply them based on the cocktail's requirements. Understanding the difference in dilution and cooling levels, along with the art of balancing flavors, is essential for creating exceptional drinks.

CHAPTER 5

GLASSWARE - PRESENTATION AND SERVICE

The choice of glassware is a fundamental element in cocktail presentation, an essential aspect of the art of mixology. Besides the visual aspect, glassware plays a significant role in the tactile perception of the experience. Each type of glass offers a unique feel and can influence the overall perception of the cocktail.

MARTINI GLASS

This elegant inverted cone-shaped glass is ideal for Martinis and other refined drinks. The shape helps keep the cocktail cold without adding ice, preserving the flavor's integrity.

MARTINI COUPE

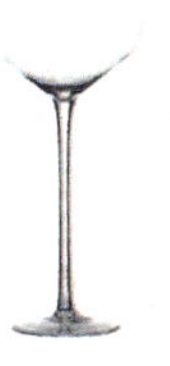

The wide bowl of the Martini Coupe allows for easy swirling and admiring the drink's colors and clarity, and the stem ensures that your hand's warmth doesn't affect the temperature of the cocktail

COLLINS GLASS

A tall and narrow glass, perfect for cocktails like the Tom Collins or Mojito. The shape helps maintain the cocktail's temperature and balance. The smooth surface is perfect for clear hand-cut crystal ice cubes, adding a touch of tactile sophistication.

LOWBALL GLASS (OLD FASHIONED)

This is the classic glass for cocktails like the Old Fashioned, Whiskey Sour, or Negroni. The wide and low shape allows for the addition of ice and even mixing of ingredients. The textured or textured surface can offer a tactile sensation that enhances the experience.

COGNAC GLASS

Ideal for cocktails served without ice but that require a larger glass, such as the Brandy Alexander or Sidecar. The shape helps concentrate aromas and flavors. The smooth inner surface can enhance the cocktail's details.

COPPER MUG

The copper mug is often used for the Moscow Mule, adding a rustic touch and emphasising the cocktail's freshness. The copper surface can provide a unique tactile sensation when holding the glass.

WHISKEY GLASS

This tumbler-shaped glass is perfect for serving whiskey, bourbon, or scotch on the rocks. The wide shape allows you to appreciate the aromas of aged whiskeys. The smooth or textured surface can influence the tactile perception of the glass.

BALLOON GLASS

This bulbous glass has become popular for serving cocktails like the Gin & Tonic. The shape provides enough space to add ice and aromatic garnishes like juniper berries and slices of lime or lemon. The smooth or decorated surface can influence both the visual and tactile aspects of the glass.

HURRICANE GLASS

This tulip-shaped glass is traditionally used for tropical cocktails like the Hurricane and Zombie. Its unique shape offers an engaging visual and gustatory experience. The worked surface can contribute to the sensory experience.

MARGARITA GLASS

This cone-shaped glass is perfect for serving Margaritas and other tequila-based cocktails. The shape allows for the concentration of agave aromas. The worked inner surface can add a unique tactile touch.

SHOT GLASS

This small glass is ideal for serving shots of spirits or strong liquor-based cocktails. It is often used for cocktails like the Tequila Sunrise or Kamikaze. The compact shape is perfect for quick consumption and intense sensory experiences.

FLUTE GLASS

This elongated glass is the classic choice for sparkling cocktails like the Champagne Cocktail or Bellini. The slim shape allows you to fully appreciate the effervescence and aromas.

WINE GLASS

A white wine glass can be used for light cocktails like the Spritz or Pimm's Cup. The shape allows you to appreciate delicate flavors. The smooth or textured surface can influence both the visual and tactile aspects of the glass.

The type of glass can vary depending on the type of cocktail you are serving and the message you want to convey.

A completely transparent glass, without designs, can highlight a hand-cut clear crystal ice cube, while a glass with a particular texture can offer a unique tactile sensation, further enriching the sensory experience.

FORBES STANDARD

Furthermore, it is essential to follow a presentation standard: cocktails with clear spirits, such as Vodka Soda or Gin and Tonic, are traditionally served in tall glasses to maintain effervescence and freshness.

On the other hand, cocktails with dark spirits mixed, such as Rum and Cola or Whiskey Ginger Ale, are often served in low glasses to emphasize the complex flavors of aged liquors.

CHAPTER 6
BALANCING INGREDIENTS IN COCKTAILS

[2:1:1]

The 2:1:1 rule is a classic guideline that can serve as an excellent starting point for many cocktails, but it's important to remember that it's not a rigid formula.

HERE'S A BREAKDOWN OF THE [2:1:1] RULE WITH A PRACTICAL EXAMPLE

SPIRIT - 2 PARTS

The spirit serves as the base and backbone of your cocktail. It provides the alcoholic strength and often imparts some of its unique flavors to the drink.

IN THE 2:1:1 FORMULA, YOU'LL USE TWICE AS MUCH SPIRIT AS THE OTHER COMPONENTS.

For example, if you're making a classic Daiquiri:

2 oz (60 ml) White Rum (the spirit)

LIQUEUR - 1 PART

Liqueurs add sweetness, depth, and sometimes a specific flavor to the cocktail. They complement the spirit and help to balance the overall taste.

IN THE 2:1:1 FORMULA, YOU'LL USE HALF AS MUCH LIQUEUR AS THE SPIRIT.

Daiquiri example:

1 oz (30 ml) Triple Sec or simple syrup (the liqueur)

FLAVORING COMPONENT - 1 PART

This component adds a burst of flavor, typically in the form of juices, citrus, or other non-alcoholic elements. It provides the freshness and acidity to brighten up the cocktail.

IN THE 2:1:1 FORMULA, YOU'LL USE AN EQUAL AMOUNT OF THE FLAVORING COMPONENT COMPARED TO THE LIQUEUR.

For the Daiquiri:

1 oz (30 ml) Freshly squeezed lime juice (the flavoring component)

EXAMPLE - CLASSIC DAIQUIRI

2 oz White Rum (the spirit)

1 oz Triple Sec (the liqueur)

1 oz Freshly squeezed lime juice (the flavoring component)

This simple, classic cocktail follows the 2:1:1 rule, creating a well-balanced, zesty, and slightly sweet drink. However, remember that the 2:1:1 rule is not absolute. It's a guideline to help you get started, but you should always taste your cocktails and adjust the ratios based on your preferences and the specific ingredients you're using.

In practice, you might find that some cocktails benefit from more or less sweetness, acidity, or alcohol content.

CHAPTER 7
MASTERING CUSTOM COCKTAILS

In the world of mixology, the art of creating custom cocktails is a true mark of distinction. This chapter offers comprehensive guidelines and advanced insights to empower you on your journey to becoming a master mixologist.

THE WORLD OF SIGNATURE COCKTAILS

Creating signature cocktails is an exploration of innovation and craftsmanship. It's about breaking free from tradition and venturing into the limitless realm of unique creations. This chapter equips you with the knowledge to unleash your creative potential and transcend the boundaries of conventional mixology.

UNDERSTANDING COCKTAIL CATEGORIES - BEYOND TRADITION

Step beyond classic cocktails and familiarize yourself with various categories like long drinks, short drinks, tropical, sours, and more. This understanding provides a solid foundation for your creative endeavors.

BALANCING INGREDIENTS - THE KEY TO COMPLEXITY

Achieving the perfect balance is the core of crafting memorable cocktails. While the 2:1:1 rule (spirit: liqueur: flavoring component) is an excellent starting point, don't hesitate to experiment and fine-tune the balance to achieve your desired flavors.

UTILIZING INFUSIONS - ELEVATING COMPLEXITY

Elevate your cocktail repertoire by experimenting with herb, spice, or fruit infusions in your spirits or homemade syrups. These infusions add layers of complexity to your creations, setting them apart from the ordinary.

CREATING SIGNATURE SYRUPS - A FLAVORFUL SIGNATURE

Dive into the world of customization by crafting signature syrups. Whether it's a black pepper syrup for a spicy kick or a vanilla coffee syrup for a hint of sophistication, these unique syrups add distinctive notes to your drinks.

ADVANCED TOOLS - THE SECRET TO CRAFTSMANSHIP

Guidelines: Expand your mixology toolkit by mastering advanced tools. Foam siphons, glass straws for precise layering, and cookie cutters for creating decorative shapes with fruits and vegetables are your allies in crafting visually stunning and innovative cocktails.

THE ART OF COCKTAIL HISTORY - WHERE TRADITION MEETS INNOVATION

To create the future, you must understand the past. Delve into the rich history of cocktails, explore their origins, and uncover the stories behind the classics. This historical knowledge will not only inspire you but also provide a foundation for creating new interpretations and pushing the boundaries of mixology.

STAYING IN TUNE WITH MIXOLOGY TRENDS AND CUSTOMER PREFERENCES

As a mixologist, it's imperative to stay current with the latest mixology trends and the promotional activities of brands in your area. Attend workshops, join industry-related groups, and participate in tastings to remain at the forefront of your craft.

UNDERSTANDING CUSTOMER PALATES

Mastering the art of interpreting your customer's taste is key. Engage with your customers, ask questions, and actively listen to their preferences. Offer suggestions based on their flavor preferences and guide them through the menu to enhance their experience.

CLASSIC COCKTAILS AS A SOURCE OF INSPIRATION

Guidelines: A profound knowledge of classic cocktails and their recipes serves as a wellspring of inspiration. Understand the time-tested combinations of liquors, spirits, and flavors in classics. This knowledge equips you with the insight to create innovative twists and unique concoctions.

In your journey to craft custom cocktails, remember that mixology is an art, and innovation is your tool. By understanding the fundamentals, and drawing inspiration from history, you can become a true maestro of mixology, creating cocktails that are as unique as they are unforgettable.

CHAPTER 8
CUSTOMER SERVICE AND COMMUNICATION IN MIXOLOGY

In the world of mixology, customer service is not just a complementary element; it's an integral part of crafting extraordinary experiences. This chapter delves into key aspects of creating lasting connections with your patrons.

EFFECTIVE COMMUNICATION - THE CORNERSTONE OF CUSTOMER RELATIONS

THE POWER OF LISTENING

Effective communication is the foundation of outstanding customer service. It's not just about talking but also about listening attentively to your patrons. Ask open-ended questions to understand their preferences, moods, and expectations.

CUSTOMER RECOMMENDATIONS - GUIDING THE EXPERIENCE

PERSONALIZED SUGGESTIONS

Utilize your knowledge of the customer's preferences to offer tailored recommendations. If they favor light and fruity cocktails, suggest a delightful Bellini that aligns perfectly with their taste.

TIME MANAGEMENT - THE ART OF EFFICIENCY

STREAMLINING YOUR WORKFLOW

Efficient time management is vital during service. Maintain a clean and organized bar, ensuring all ingredients and tools are within easy reach. An organized workspace leads to quicker and more precise service.

SATISFACTION CHECK - ENSURING DELIGHT

ENSURING HAPPINESS

After serving a drink, make it a habit to check for customer satisfaction. A simple inquiry like "Is everything to your liking?" or "Would you like anything else?" demonstrates your commitment to their enjoyment.

BAR KNOWLEDGE: MASTERY OF YOUR DOMAIN

KNOWING YOUR BAR INSIDE OUT

To deliver exceptional service, you must be intimately familiar with your bar. Know the exact locations of ingredients and tools. This knowledge empowers you to provide swift and accurate service.

UPSELLING - ENHANCING THE EXPERIENCE

THE ART OF SUGGESTION

Utilize your training to enhance the customer's experience. Suggest premium cocktails, unique creations, or exclusive spirits that align with their preferences.

CUSTOMER LOYALTY - BUILDING LASTING RELATIONSHIPS

GOING BEYOND TRANSACTIONS

Strive to create an extraordinary experience that entices customers to return regularly. Go the extra mile by learning their names and recalling their preferences. This not only fosters loyalty but also deepens your connection with your patrons.

THE PSYCHOLOGY OF MIXOLOGY - UNDERSTANDING CUSTOMER BEHAVIOR

GRASPING CUSTOMER PSYCHOLOGY

Dive into the psychology of mixology and gain insight into customer behavior. Tailor your service and recommendations based on their emotional state, mood, and expectations.

FORBES FIVE-STAR STANDARDS - PURSUIT OF EXCELLENCE

SETTING THE HIGHEST BENCHMARK

Embrace the Forbes Five-Star service standards as your guide to delivering excellence in every aspect of your customer service. These rigorous benchmarks will steer you towards the zenith of hospitality.

The philosophy of "Ichi-go Ichi-e" in Japanese culture emphasizes the uniqueness and impermanence of each moment. When applied to mixology and bartending, it means that every interaction with a customer is a one-of-a-kind opportunity to create a memorable experience. By embodying this philosophy, mixologists and bartenders recognize that each customer is unique, and each cocktail is a chance to make a lasting connection. They focus on delivering impeccable service, sharing their knowledge, and making tailored recommendations to ensure that every patron feels valued and special, fostering loyalty and leaving a lasting impression that goes beyond the ordinary.

CHAPTER 9
THE ART OF ICE IN COCKTAILS

Ice is a fundamental element in crafting the perfect cocktail, influencing far more than just temperature control. It plays a pivotal role in dilution, texture, presentation, and even flavor.

VARIETIES OF ICE TO ELEVATE THE COCKTAIL EXPERIENCE

Cubed Ice

The classic and versatile choice, ideal for shaken cocktails. It cools the mixture rapidly and keeps it cold during service, introducing minimal dilution.

Crushed Ice

Crafted by breaking cubed ice into small pieces, it's the preferred option for cocktails like the Mint Julep or Daiquiri. The crushed consistency elevates the tactile sensation and aesthetics.

Spherical Ice

Prized for its elegance, spherical ice is created using specialized molds. Perfect for low glasses like the Old Fashioned, it maintains the drink's chill without overly diluting it.

Cuboid or Column Ice

Typically employed for cocktails such as the Tom Collins or Highball, this elongated shape preserves the drink's temperature and balance.

Large Cubed Ice

Designed for rock glasses, like for Old Fashioned and Negroni. These larger cubes melt more slowly, preserving the drink's freshness and flavors. Best choice of ice when serving sipping and expensive spirits.

THE SIGNIFICANCE OF ICE PURITY

Ice purity is paramount. Opt for ice made with purified or demineralized water to prevent unwanted flavors or odors from compromising the cocktail. Some establishments invest in specific water filtration systems to ensure high-quality ice, a testament to their commitment to excellence.

ICE SHAPES AND JAPANESE INFLUENCE

Japanese culture has contributed significantly to the art of ice preparation. Some Japanese bars are renowned for their perfectly clear ice spheres. Achieving this level of perfection demands meticulous attention to detail and the use of purified water. A cocktail served with Japanese ice signifies a high degree of craftsmanship and quality, capturing the essence of precision.

THE SCIENCE OF ICE DILUTION

The rate of ice dilution in a cocktail is a pivotal factor in achieving the desired flavor profile. Understand that the duration of contact between ice and the mixture influences dilution. Shaking a cocktail with cubed ice, for example, leads to less dilution compared to drinks prepared directly in a glass with column ice. A skilled mixologist comprehends the importance of balancing dilution to create the perfect cocktail.

ELEVATING PRESENTATION THROUGH ICE

Ice isn't merely functional; it significantly contributes to cocktail presentation. Selecting the appropriate ice shape enhances the visual appeal of your drink. An ice sphere in an Old Fashioned glass or an ice column in a Highball glass adds an extra layer of sophistication.91

CHOOSING ICE WISELY

Recognize that each cocktail necessitates specific types of ice to strike the perfect equilibrium between temperature and dilution. Your choice of ice should align with the cocktail you're crafting and the preferences of your clientele. In doing so, you demonstrate an elevated level of dedication and expertise that significantly influences the quality of your creations.

CONTEMPORARY TRENDS AND ADDITIONAL INSIGHTS

Fruit-Infused Ice

An emerging trend involves using ice infused with fresh fruit, imparting fruity notes to cocktails without the need for added syrups.

Edible Flower Ice

Some top-tier bars experiment with edible flowers encapsulated in ice, adding a touch of visual elegance and a subtle floral aroma to drinks.

Green Tea Ice

Green tea ice cubes have gained popularity due to their earthy flavor and antioxidant properties. They are frequently used in cocktails to infuse depth and a hint of healthiness.

Mint and Basil Ice

Adding mint or basil leaves to the water before freezing creates ice cubes that add refreshing herbal notes to cocktails.

CHAPTER 10
BAR STATION SETUP – THE ART OF ORGANIZATION

In the world of mixology, the organization of your bar station is a cornerstone of efficient cocktail preparation. Just as a chef depends on an organized kitchen, a well-structured bar station is vital for a mixologist.

THE IMPORTANCE OF ORGANIZATION FOR MIXOLOGISTS

Organization is the backbone of an efficient bar station. It minimizes the time spent searching for ingredients and tools, optimizes your efficiency, and guarantees a smooth and timely service for your customers.

HYGIENE AND SAFETY

Regular cleaning and sanitization are fundamental. Ensure all work surfaces, tools, and refrigerators are thoroughly cleaned to maintain a pristine and safe environment for cocktail preparation.

THE SPEED RACK

The speed rack, housing the most frequently used base liquor bottles, should be strategically positioned for quick access, minimizing the time spent searching and maximizing productivity for mixologists.

GARNISHES AND FRUIT PLACEMENT

One of the key elements of preparing your cocktail station is the artful placement of fruit and garnishes. These finishing touches not only contribute to the visual appeal of your cocktails but also enhance their aroma and flavor. Here are some tips on how to expertly place fruit and garnishes:

Citrus Twists

To craft a citrus twist, you'll need a sharp knife or a channel knife. Carefully cut a thin strip of zest from a citrus fruit, like a lemon or an orange. Gently twist it over the cocktail to release its aromatic oils. You can position the twist on the rim of the glass or let it float on the drink's surface, typically near the garnish area of your cocktail station.

Cocktail Cherries

Maraschino cherries are a classic garnish for many cocktails. Skewer one or more cherries on a cocktail pick or a decorative stirrer and place them in the drink. They can rest at the bottom of the glass or be perched on the rim, usually in a designated cherry container.

Olives

If you're preparing a cocktail like a Martini, use a cocktail pick to skewer one or more olives. You can position the olives on the rim or drop them directly into the drink, within easy reach of your garnish station.

Herbs and Leaves

Fresh herbs like mint, basil, or a sprig of rosemary can add delightful aroma and flavor to your cocktails. Place them on the rim of the glass or gently float a leaf on the drink's surface, near the herbs and leaves section of your station.

Umbrella Picks and Cocktail Swords

These whimsical and decorative accessories are perfect for tropical and playful cocktails. Use them to infuse a lighthearted touch into your creations by placing the umbrella or sword on the rim or letting it float within the drink, usually near your playful garnish area.

Edible Flowers

Edible flowers are not only a feast for the eyes but also for the palate. They contribute both beauty and a unique flavor to your cocktails. Gently let them float on the drink's surface or use them as a final flourish for presentation, which is commonly near the edible flowers section.

Straws and Swizzle Sticks

Colorful straws or swizzle sticks are not just practical tools for sipping but also vibrant decorative elements. Insert them into the cocktail for easy sipping while adding a vibrant burst of color, near the straw and swizzle stick holder.

Essential Fruits and Ingredients

In addition to these garnishes, some essential fruits and ingredients should be on hand at your cocktail station. Oranges, lemons, limes, ginger, mint, basil, rosemary, and ginger are versatile and often-used components for both garnishes and cocktail ingredients. Don't forget dried fruits, which can be used to create flavorful infusions and garnishes, typically in the essential fruit and ingredients area of your station.

LOGICAL PLACEMENT

Logical organization means positioning fresh juices near your cocktail preparation area, keeping spirits within easy reach, and making garnishes readily accessible at your workspace. This setup creates a seamless workflow for mixologists.

WORKSTATION SETUP

Your bar station should feature a well-defined workspace equipped with all the essential tools for mixologists: shakers, jiggers, muddlers, bar spoons, strainers, and utensils for cutting fruit.

REFRIGERATOR MANAGEMENT

Maintain well-organized refrigerators and label containers for ingredients like juices, syrups, and dairy products. Separate refrigerators for dairy and fresh fruits prevent flavor transfer. Regularly clean your refrigerators to prevent mold growth and unpleasant odors. Check ingredient expiration dates and remove any expired items.

BAR MAT AND BAR TOWEL PLACEMENT

Place bar mats in areas where you handle liquids, such as in front of draft beer taps, and ensure bar towels are readily available for quickly wiping spills and maintaining general hygiene during cocktail preparation.

OPENING AND CLOSING PROCEDURES

Opening

Start your shift with a clean, well-organized station. Check ingredient levels, refill containers, and ensure all tools are in place.

Closing

End your shift by restoring the station to its initial state. Clean all tools, check ingredient levels again, and securely cover bottles. Properly dispose of waste and sanitize work surfaces.

ORGANIZING YOUR LIQUOR CABINET

An organized liquor cabinet is not only about efficiency but also enhances the visual appeal of your bar area. It streamlines cocktail preparation and elevates the overall customer experience.

POSITIONING BOTTLES - VISUAL PSYCHOLOGY

Dedicate the top shelf to premium and frequently used liquors, drawing attention to your best spirits and creating a visual focal point in your bar station.

CATEGORISATION - SIMPLIFYING ACCESS

Arrange bottles by categories (vodka, whiskey, rum, gin, tequila, and liqueurs) to ensure quick and easy access to the right spirit for each cocktail.

FREQUENTLY USED BOTTLES - CONVENIENCE AT ARM'S REACH

Keep frequently used bottles at eye level and within easy reach. This includes popular liquors, mixers, and bitters, ensuring convenience while crafting cocktails.

LABELLING AND ORDER - PRESENTATION IS KEY

Neatly labeled bottles with outward-facing labels offer a professional and organised appearance, making identification effortless. Group similar bottles and arrange them logically based on their common use in cocktails.

A well-organized bar station and liquor cabinet are vital for mixologists. They increase efficiency and enhance the overall customer experience. cleanliness, and readiness for the next shift, translating into high-quality cocktails and satisfied customers.

CHAPTER 11
MASTERING MIXOLOGY TOOLS

To truly excel in the art of mixology, it's essential to have a deep understanding of the tools of the trade. Each tool serves as an extension of your creativity and expertise, allowing you to unlock new dimensions of flavor and presentation. Let's dive into each mixology tool, exploring their functions, historical significance, and how they are used to craft various types of cocktails.

SHAKERS

TWO-PIECE SHAKER (BOSTON SHAKER)

Function

The Boston Shaker, comprising a metal or glass tumbler and a snug-fitting top lid, is perfect for cocktails that require vigorous shaking, such as the Margarita, Espresso Martini, and many others.

Historical Tidbit

The Boston Shaker has been a fixture in cocktail culture for over a century. Its simplicity and efficiency make it a favorite among bartenders worldwide.

THREE-PIECE SHAKER (COBBLER SHAKER)

Function

The Cobbler Shaker features three parts: a main tumbler, a lid with an integrated strainer, and an upper cap. It's ideal for cocktails that need vigorous shaking and precise straining, such as the Daiquiri, or any drink where you want to accurately strain ingredients like fruit pieces or crushed ice.

Curious Fact

The three-piece Cobbler Shaker gained popularity during the mid-19th century, offering a compact design with a built-in strainer. Its elegance and functionality have made it a classic choice for many cocktails.

PARISIAN SHAKER (FRENCH SHAKER)

Function

The Parisian Shaker, often referred to as the French Shaker, is a bar tool used for mixing cocktails. It consists of two main components: a large metal tin and a smaller metal tin. Bartenders use the Parisian Shaker by placing ingredients and ice in the smaller tin, then sealing it with the larger tin and shaking vigorously. The primary function of this shaker is to quickly and thoroughly mix the ingredients in a cocktail. While it doesn't have a built-in strainer like the Cobbler Shaker, a separate Hawthorne strainer or fine mesh strainer is typically used to strain the drink when pouring it into a glass.

Curious Fact

The Parisian Shaker is known for its simplicity and versatility. It is often favored by professional bartenders for its ease of use and durability. While it may not have the built-in strainer of the Cobbler Shaker, it has remained a classic tool in the world of mixology and is a preferred choice for many bartenders for crafting a wide range of cocktails.

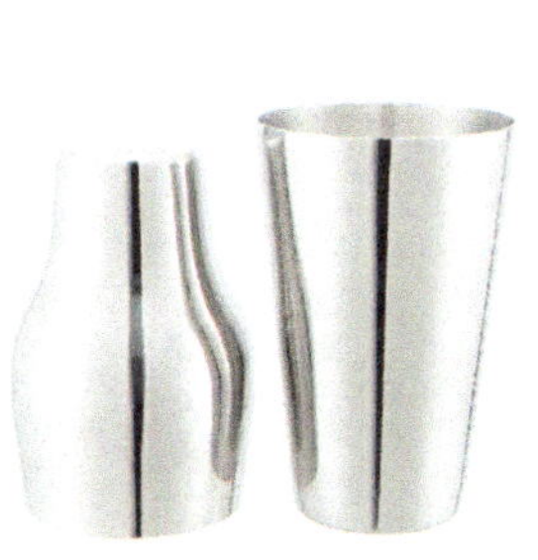

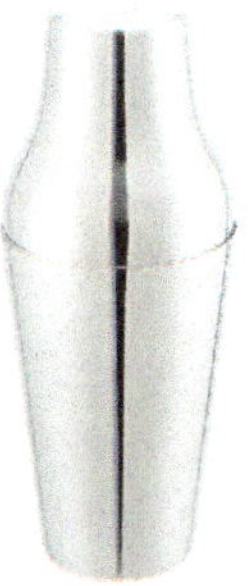

MIXING GLASS

Function

The mixing glass, or stirring glass, is ideal for cocktails that require stirring rather than vigorous shaking, such as the Martini, Negroni and Manhattan. Stirring in the mixing glass avoids the aggressive shaking that could cause excessive foam or crushed ice and help to control the dilution of ice in the drink.

Historical Tidbit

The mixing glass has a storied past, evolving from early cut-crystal designs to more modern tempered glass versions. It's a tool that connects mixologists to the traditions of the past while embracing contemporary mixing techniques.

STRAINERS

Function

Strainers are essential tools for separating the cocktail from ice chips or other solid ingredients. There are different types, each with specific applications:

Curiosity

Strainers are not just practical tools; they are also a testament to the precision and attention to detail that bartenders bring to their craft. The choice of strainer can influence the overall aesthetics and quality of a cocktail.

HAWTHORN STRAINER

Ideal for cocktails shaken in a shaker, like the Daiquiri or Margarita, providing effective straining.

JULEP STRAINER

Often used in combination with the mixing glass to strain the stirred cocktail without ice into cocktail or coupe glasses.

FINE MESH STRAINER

Perfect for cocktails like the Martini or Negroni, where the presence of small unwanted particles could compromise the cocktail's perfection.

BAR SPOONS

Function

Bar spoons are essential tools for mixing and layering cocktails with precision. They typically have long, spiral handles with various types of terminations. The design of bar spoons allows bartenders to effortlessly stir and combine ingredients in a mixing glass, ensuring that the flavors meld harmoniously. Additionally, some bar spoons feature muddlers on the opposite end, making them versatile tools for both stirring and muddling ingredients.

Curious Fact

Bar spoons have a long history in the world of cocktails and mixology. Their unique design, often with a twisted handle for easier stirring, has been refined over the years for optimal functionality. The long handles also allow bartenders to reach the bottom of taller glasses, ensuring a thorough mixing process. In addition to their practical use, bar spoons are often chosen for their aesthetic appeal, as they can add a touch of elegance to the cocktail-making process.

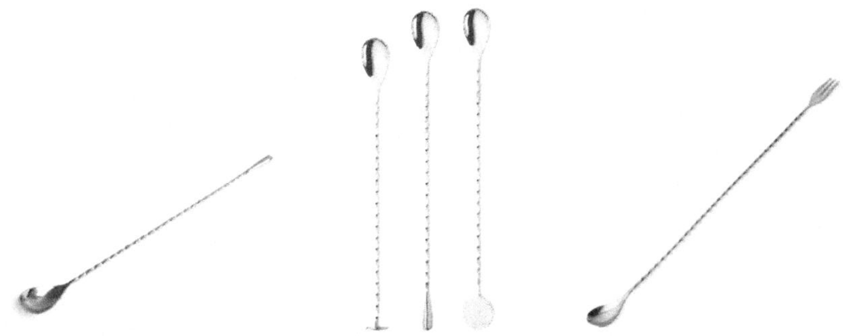

MUDDLER

Function

The muddler is a vital tool in the bartender's arsenal, used for extracting essential oils, flavors, and aromas from ingredients like mint leaves, fruit, or sugar. It's particularly important in cocktails like the Mojito, Caipirinha, or Old Fashioned, where muddling is necessary to release the full potential of the ingredients.

Curious Fact

The muddler's history can be traced back to the early days of mixology. Its design has evolved over time, with contemporary muddlers typically made of wood or stainless steel. The muddling process not only imparts flavor but also adds a tactile and sensory element to the cocktail-making experience. Muddlers are available in various styles, from simple, single-piece designs to more ornate and decorative options, reflecting the artistry and craftsmanship in mixology.

JIGGERS

Function

Jiggers are indispensable tools used for accurate measurement in cocktail preparation. They come in various sizes and typically have two separate measuring cups, one on each end, to provide precise measurements of spirits, liqueurs, and other cocktail ingredients. Jiggers ensure that each cocktail is consistently well-balanced and maintains the intended flavor profile.

Curious Fact

The use of jiggers for cocktail measurement dates back to the early days of bartending. Before the widespread use of jiggers, bartenders often relied on various improvised methods to measure ingredients, such as counting seconds or using bar tools like shot glasses. The introduction of jiggers revolutionized the precision of cocktail making, contributing to the standardization of recipes and consistency in the world of mixology. Today, jiggers continue to be an essential tool for both professional bartenders and home enthusiasts, ensuring that every cocktail is crafted with meticulous accuracy.

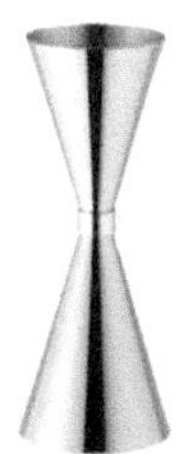
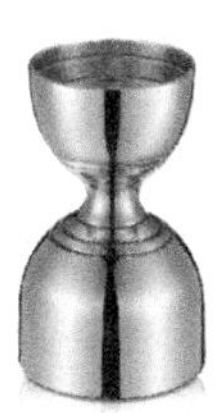

OUNCE (OZ) AND MILLILITRE (ML) EXPLANATION

Jiggers are marked with both ounce (oz) and millilitre (ml) measurements, making them versatile for international and local cocktail recipes. An ounce is a unit of volume commonly used in the United States, while the millilitre is the standard unit of volume in the metric system.

Ounce (oz)

In the United States, an ounce is equal to approximately 29.57 millilitres. Jiggers are often marked with ounce measurements ranging from 1/4 oz to 2 oz, allowing bartenders to accurately measure and pour the appropriate amount of each ingredient according to the recipe.

Milliliter (ml)

The millilitre is the metric unit of volume, and it is widely used in many parts of the world. Jiggers marked with millilitre measurements provide a more precise way to follow cocktail recipes that use the metric system. Common millilitre measurements on jiggers range from 5 ml to 60 ml or more.

PEELERS

Function:

Peelers, including citrus peelers, are essential tools in cocktail preparation. They are used for efficiently removing the zest or peel from various fruits, primarily citrus fruits like lemons, limes, and oranges. The importance of peelers in cocktails lies in their ability to extract the flavorful and aromatic oils found in the fruit's peel, enhancing the taste and aroma of the drinks. Here, we will explore different types of peelers used in bartending:

DIFFERENT TYPES OF PEELERS:

- **Standard Citrus Zester:** This peeler typically has a long, slender design with sharp, small holes that effectively remove zest from citrus fruits. It's excellent for creating fine strips or shavings of zest, which can be used for garnishing cocktails.
- **Channel Knife or Citrus Stripper:** Channel knives have a blade with a V-shaped groove. They are used to create decorative citrus twists or garnishes by cutting a spiral strip of zest. The twisted zest can be hung on the rim of a cocktail glass, adding visual appeal.
- **Y-Peeler:** Y-peelers are versatile tools that can be used for peeling the skin from various fruits. While they are not exclusive to citrus, they are efficient and easy to handle, making them a valuable addition to a bartender's toolkit.

- **Julienne Peeler:** This type of peeler creates thin, matchstick-sized strips of zest. While less common in cocktail preparation, it can be used for more decorative garnishes, adding a unique touch to certain drinks.

WHY CITRUS PEELERS ARE IMPORTANT FOR COCKTAILS:

Citrus peelers are indispensable tools in mixology because they allow bartenders to extract the aromatic and flavorful oils found in citrus zest. These oils can significantly enhance the taste and aroma of cocktails, providing a burst of citrus essence. Bartenders often express citrus oils over the surface of a cocktail, enriching its flavor and providing a delightful sensory experience for the drinker. Whether it's a classic martini with a lemon twist or a tropical cocktail with an orange zest garnish, citrus peelers help bartenders create visually appealing and aromatic cocktails that stand out in both taste and presentation.

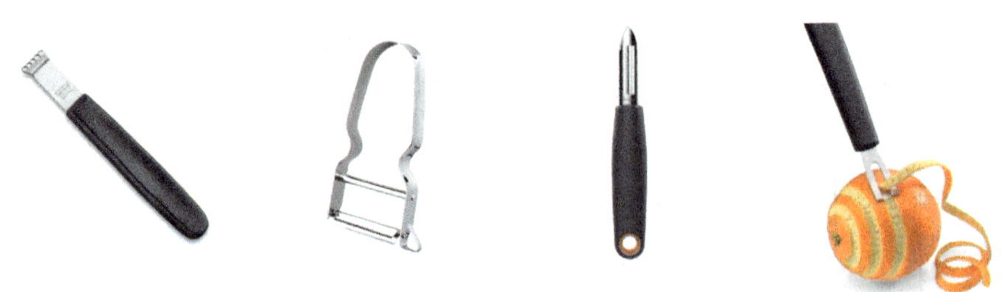

METAL POURER

Metal pourers, also known as liquor pourers or bottle pour spouts, serve a vital function in the world of bartending and beverage service. These small, typically metal, devices are designed to control the flow of liquid from a bottle, ensuring consistent and accurate pours of spirits and other liquids. Here's some information about metal pourers and a curious fact about their usage:

Function

Metal pourers are designed to fit securely into the neck of a liquor bottle, replacing the bottle's original cap or cork. They typically consist of a spout or nozzle made of metal and a rubber or plastic stopper to create an airtight seal.

The primary functions of metal pourers include:

- **Precision Pouring:** Metal pourers are designed to deliver a controlled and consistent stream of liquid when the bottle is tipped. This helps bartenders measure out accurate quantities of spirits, which is crucial for creating well-balanced cocktails.
- **Reduced Spillage:** By controlling the flow of liquid, pourers minimize spillage and prevent over-pouring, which is not only wasteful but can also affect the taste and quality of a drink.

- **Improved Hygiene:** Pourers keep the bottle's contents protected from external contaminants, such as dust or fruit flies, while still allowing for efficient pouring.
- **Speed and Efficiency:** Bartenders can work more efficiently with pourers, as they eliminate the need to repeatedly open and close bottle caps or corks.

Curious Fact:

The use of metal pourers has significantly contributed to the professionalization of the bartending industry. Before the widespread adoption of pourers, bartenders often had to free-pour, relying on their instincts and pouring skills to measure out the correct amount of alcohol. This method was highly subjective and could result in inconsistent drinks.

The introduction of metal pourers brought precision and consistency to the bar, making it easier for bartenders to create cocktails with the exact measurements required for a particular recipe. This not only improved the quality of cocktails but also reduced the likelihood of over-pouring.

CHAPTER 12
MODERN MIXOLOGY TECHNIQUES

In recent years, the art of mixology has been invigorated by the integration of innovative culinary techniques and tools. These approaches infuse cocktails with unique flavors, presentations, and textures, taking your mixology game to the next level.

VACUUM INFUSION

DESCRIPTION

The vacuum infusion technique, popularized by renowned mixologist Tony Conigliaro, applies principles from culinary sous-vide. By removing the air from the infusion environment, it accelerates flavor extraction and mingling of ingredients.

Select Your Ingredients: Choose the ingredients you want to infuse into your spirits. This can range from herbs and fruits to spices and botanicals.

Vacuum-Seal the Ingredients: Place the selected ingredients in a vacuum-sealable bag, ensuring a tight seal.

Extract the Air: Use a vacuum machine to remove air from the bag. As the air pressure decreases, the ingredients rapidly absorb the liquid (whether it's a spirit or a syrup).

Allow the Infusion: Let the vacuum-sealed bag sit for a specific time (usually a few hours) to let the flavors meld together.

Strain and Use: Once the infusion process is complete, strain the liquid to remove any solid ingredients, leaving you with a concentrated infusion to use in your cocktails.

RESULT

Vacuum infusion yields highly concentrated and vibrant flavor infusions in a fraction of the time it would take with traditional methods. This technique is ideal for infusing spirits with botanicals, spices, or fruits for complex and distinctive cocktail bases.

WHEN TO USE

Use vacuum infusion when you want to create intense and distinctive flavor profiles in your cocktails efficiently. It's excellent for crafting unique and complex bases for various cocktails.

SOUS VIDE FOR HOMEMADE INGREDIENTS

DESCRIPTION

Sous vide cooking has found its place in mixology, particularly for crafting homemade infusions and syrups.

Combine Ingredients: Place the desired ingredients (e.g., fruits, spices, herbs) in a vacuum-sealable bag or jar. Add a base liquid such as vodka, rum, or simple syrup.

Seal and Cook: Vacuum-seal the bag or use a jar with a vacuum seal attachment. Set your sous vide machine to the desired temperature and cook time.

Infusion Process: The sous vide process infuses the base liquid with flavors at a precise, consistent temperature.

Strain and Use: After cooking, strain the infused liquid to remove solid particles and use it in your cocktails.

RESULT

Sous vide infusions produce carefully controlled flavors, preserving the integrity of the ingredients. It's an exceptional technique for crafting infusions with balanced and nuanced tastes for cocktails.

WHEN TO USE

Utilize sous vide for homemade ingredients when you want precise control over the infusion process. It's excellent for crafting high-quality infusions and syrups with consistent flavor profiles.

SIPHON INFUSION WITH CO2

DESCRIPTION

Using a siphon with CO2 allows for rapid infusion of flavors into your cocktails.

Choose Your Ingredients: Select the ingredients you want to infuse, such as herbs, spices, or fruits.

Place Ingredients in the Siphon: Add the chosen ingredients to the siphon's container.

Charge with CO2: Charge the siphon with CO2, pressurizing the container.

Infuse: Allow the CO2 to force the infusion of the ingredients into your spirits or other liquids. The pressurization expedites the process, resulting in vibrant flavors.

Release and Strain: Release the pressure from the siphon and strain the infused liquid to remove any remaining solid particles.

RESULT

The CO2 infusion process intensifies the extraction of flavors from ingredients and provides an efficient way to incorporate unique elements into your cocktails. This technique is ideal for introducing herbaceous or botanical notes to your drinks with speed and precision.

WHEN TO USE

Use siphon infusion with CO2 when you want to add vibrant and fresh flavors to your cocktails quickly. It's excellent for infusing botanicals, herbs, or spices to create dynamic and lively flavor profiles.

FRUIT DEHYDRATOR

DESCRIPTION

A fruit dehydrator isn't just for garnishes; it's also used to create concentrated fruit flavorings. This technique dries fruits to extract their essence.

Select Your Fruits: Choose the fruits you want to dehydrate. Citrus peels are a popular choice.

Prepare the Fruits: Wash and slice the fruits to your desired thickness.

Dehydrate the Fruits: Place the prepared fruits on the dehydrator trays and set the temperature and time according to the manufacturer's instructions.

Create Fruit Powders: Once the fruits are thoroughly dehydrated, you can turn them into powders by using a spice grinder or a mortar and pestle. These powders can be used for garnishes, rimming salts, or to add intense aromatics to your cocktails.

RESULT

Dehydrated fruits offer intense and concentrated flavors that elevate your cocktails. They can be used for rimming glasses, garnishes, or as a flavorful ingredient to provide layers of taste in your drinks.

WHEN TO USE

Use the fruit dehydrator when you want to intensify the fruit flavors in your cocktails without adding excess moisture. It's excellent for creating garnishes with a powerful aroma.

DRY ICE (SOLID CO2)

DESCRIPTION

Dry ice, or solid CO2, has become an innovative tool for mixologists to create unique presentations and chilling effects.

Handle with Care: Always use gloves or tongs when handling dry ice to avoid contact with bare skin.

Chill Effect: Place a small chunk of dry ice in a drink to create a mesmerizing, foggy effect. Ensure the customer is aware of the presence of dry ice, and don't allow them to consume it.

Storage and Safety: Store dry ice in an insulated container and use it as needed. Be aware of safety precautions, such as adequate ventilation when using dry ice.

RESULT

By adding small chunks of dry ice to your cocktails, you create a dramatic, visually engaging, and chilling effect. This technique enhances the overall sensory experience of your drinks, making them memorable for your patrons.

WHEN TO USE

Use dry ice to add a touch of drama and a chilling effect to your cocktails, enhancing their visual appeal and sensory experience.

WHIPPING SIPHON FOR FOAMS AND CARBONATION

DESCRIPTION

The whipping siphon is a versatile tool for creating foams and carbonating cocktails. It can be used to carbonate a wide range of liquids, from spirits to juices and syrups.

Prepare Ingredients: Combine your desired cocktail ingredients for the foam or carbonated drink.

Pour into Siphon: Pour the cocktail mixture into the whipping siphon's canister. Charge it with CO2 cartridges to carbonate or nitrous oxide (N2O) for foaming.

Dispense: Dispense the foam or carbonated cocktail as needed. Adjust the pressure to control the level of carbonation or foam density.

RESULT

The whipping siphon allows mixologists to craft light and frothy foams for the top of cocktails, enhancing their texture and appearance. Additionally, it enables precise carbonation, resulting in effervescent and bubbly drinks.

WHEN TO USE

Employ the whipping siphon for foams and carbonation when you want to introduce new textures and carbonation levels to your cocktails, enhancing their overall drinking experience.

BLOWTORCHES

DESCRIPTION

While traditionally associated with culinary tasks like caramelizing sugar, blowtorches have found their way into mixology. Mixologists use blowtorches to impart smoky or toasted flavors to ingredients like fruit or herbs. These tools elevate cocktails by adding intriguing charred notes.

RESULT

These torched ingredients add intriguing and complex charred notes to cocktails, enhancing their aromatic and flavor profiles.

SMOKING TECHNIQUE INSIDE A BELL JAR

DESCRIPTION

The smoking technique inside a bell jar is a method employed by mixologists to infuse cocktails with smoky aromas and flavors. This innovative approach involves placing ingredients within a sealed bell jar and introducing smoke to create a unique and aromatic cocktail experience.

RESULT

Mixologists employ the smoking technique inside a bell jar to infuse cocktails with smoky aromas and flavors, creating a unique and aromatic cocktail experience.

ROTOVAP (ROTARY EVAPORATOR)

DESCRIPTION

The rotary evaporator, known as the rotovap, is a sophisticated piece of equipment used for distillation and concentration of flavors. Mixologists use it to extract and condense intricate and highly concentrated essences. The rotovap has become a tool for pushing the boundaries of cocktail innovation.

RESULT

Mixologists use the rotovap to extract and condense intricate and highly concentrated essences, pushing the boundaries of cocktail innovation.

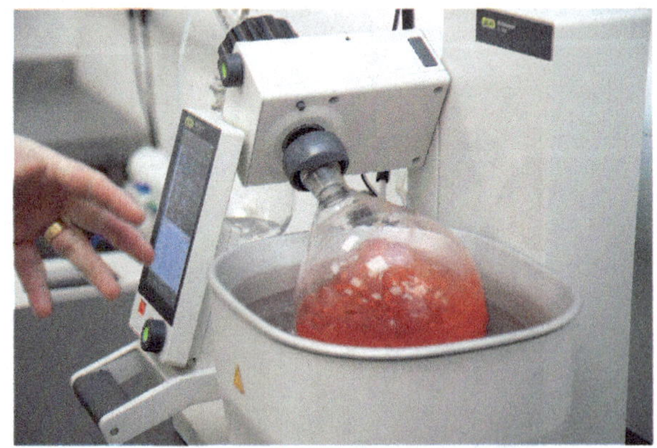

CHAPTER 11
THE WORLD OF COCKTAILS

As we delve into the world of cocktails, remember that each of these libations has a history, a tradition, and a culture of its own. They are a testament to human creativity, and their enduring popularity is a testament to their excellence.

COCKTAIL CULTURE

In this chapter, we'll delve deep into the heart of cocktail culture, exploring its rich heritage, the ingenious innovations that sprouted from necessity, and the essential elements that define a remarkable cocktail. Cocktails have endured through the annals of time, transcending epochs and evolving with the changing tides of history.

THE ART OF MASKING SPIRITS

Cocktails have a legacy that dates back centuries. They were born in an era when the quality of spirits was far from stellar. The introduction of cocktails was, in part, a solution to mask the harshness of these spirits. It was a dash of sugar, a squeeze of citrus, and a sprinkle of herbs to turn unrefined booze into a palatable, even delightful, drink. In many ways, cocktails have always been a reflection of their times.

COCKTAILS AND THE PROHIBITION ERA: SPEAKEASIES AND INNOVATION

The Prohibition era in the United States, which lasted from 1920 to 1933, is a significant chapter in cocktail history. During this period, the sale, production, and transportation of alcoholic beverages were banned. Yet, the demand for alcoholic drinks persisted. To adapt to this challenge, innovative mixologists and bootleggers created new concoctions that concealed the inferior quality of bathtub gins and moonshine. Thus, cocktails like the

Sidecar, the Bee's Knees, and the Last Word emerged from the shadows of the speakeasies.

TIMELESS CLASSICS AND CONTEMPORARY CREATIONS

Introduzione: In this chapter, you'll embark on a journey through a curated selection of timeless classics and contemporary creations. These are the cocktails that every aspiring mixologist should know by heart. They serve as the foundation upon which you can build your signature concoctions. Each cocktail embodies the principles of balance, flavor, and presentation that we've explored earlier. They are the building blocks upon which your mixology skills will flourish.

THE ART AND SCIENCE OF MIXOLOGY

As you journey through these pages, you'll uncover the secrets, stories, and techniques that will transform you from an enthusiast to a skilled mixologist. These cocktails are more than just recipes; they're a gateway to understanding a world where creativity knows no bounds and where every glass is a canvas for your imagination.

APERITIFS COCKTAILS

An aperitif cocktail family is a delightful group of drinks renowned for their unique combination of bitter and sweet flavors. These cocktails, often infused with ingredients like vermouth, Campari, and Aperol, are designed to awaken the palate and stimulate the appetite. They serve as a flavorful introduction to a meal, setting the stage for an extraordinary dining experience.

APEROL SPRITZ

Recipe: 1 ½ oz Aperol, Prosecco, Club Soda.

Preparation: Build the cocktail directly in a wine glass with ice.

Glass Type: Wine glass.

Garnish: An orange slice.

Ice Type: Cubed ice.

History: The Aperol Spritz has Italian origins and is believed to have been created in the Veneto region in the 19th century.

Curiosity: The Aperol Spritz has become an iconic summer drink in Italy, loved for its balance of bitterness, fizz, and subtle sweetness.

SPRITZ HUGO

Recipe: 1 ½ oz St Germain, Prosecco, Club Soda, Splash of Lime.

Preparation: Build the cocktail directly in a wine glass with ice.

Glass Type: Wine glass.

Garnish: A sprig of mint and a lime wedge.

Ice Type: Cubed ice.

History: The Hugo Spritz is a relatively modern creation, originating in the South Tyrol region of Italy, blending elderflower liqueur with prosecco.

Curiosity: Is a fresh and fragrant alternative to the Aperol Spritz. The elderflower liqueur imparts a distinctive floral aroma to the cocktail.

NEGRONI

Recipe: 1 oz Sweet Vermouth, 1 oz Campari, 1 oz London Dry gin.

Preparation: Stir all the ingredients with ice for 15 seconds with orange peel and serve in a low glass with a large ice cube.

Glass Type: Low glass with a large ice cube.

Garnish: Orange zest.

Ice Type: Large ice cube.

History: The Negroni is a classic Italian cocktail dating back to the early 20th century and is named after Count Camillo Negroni.

Curiosity: The combination of ingredients in the Negroni creates a unique balance of sweetness, bitterness, and herbal notes. It's a cocktail cherished by gin enthusiasts.

BELLINI

Recipe: Champagne, 1 oz Peach Puree.

Preparation: Pour the peach puree into a champagne flute and top with champagne. Gently stir.

Glass Type: Champagne flute.

Garnish: Peach slice

History: The Bellini was created at Harry's Bar in Venice in the 1930s, named after the color of a saint's toga in a painting by Giovanni Bellini.

Curiosity: The Bellini is a fruity and refreshing cocktail that highlights the flavor of ripe peaches. It's a classic champagne-based drink.

KIR ROYAL

Recipe: 5 oz Champagne or sparkling wine, 0.5 oz Crème de Cassis (blackcurrant liqueur)

Preparation: Chill a flute or wine glass. Pour the Crème de Cassis into the glass. Carefully top it up with the Champagne or sparkling wine. Gently stir to combine.

Glass Type: Flute or wine glass

Garnish: None required, but you can add a fresh blackberry or a twist of lemon.

History: Kir Royale is a delightful French aperitif that's a variation of the Kir, which is made with white wine. The Royale version adds the elegance of Champagne or sparkling wine.

MOSCOW MULE

Recipe: 2 oz Tito's Vodka, 1 oz Lime Juice, Ginger Beer.

Preparation: Serve in a copper mug with ice.

Glass Type: Copper mug.

Garnish: Mint leaves and a lime wedge.

Ice Type: Cubed ice.

History: The Moscow Mule was created in the United States in the 1940s and was one of the cocktails responsible for popularizing vodka in America.

Curiosity: The traditional copper mug not only looks great but also keeps the Moscow Mule exceptionally cold.

CLASSIC COCKTAILS

Classic cocktails stand as a timeless array of enduring drinks, celebrated for their simplicity and lasting charm. From the Martini to the Old Fashioned, these libations combine spirits and mixers with refined elegance. They epitomize the art of mixology at its purest, a nod to tradition, and a testament to expertly crafted beverages' timeless appeal.

GIN OR VODKA MARTINI

Recipe: 2 ½ oz Vodka or Gin, 1/2 oz Dry Vermouth.

Preparation: Stir the ingredients with ice and lemon zest for 15 seconds and serve in a chilled martini glass.

Glass Type: Chilled martini glass.

Garnish: Olives and a lemon twist.

History: The Martini has a long history, but the classic Gin Martini is said to have been created in the late 19th century.

Curiosity: Stirring a Martini, rather than shaking it, can create a smoother, clearer cocktail. The choice between gin and vodka allows for different flavor profiles.

DRY MARTINI
(MORE GIN/VODKA AND LESS VERMOUTH)

Recipe: 2 ½ oz Gin, 1/4 oz Dry Vermouth

Preparation: Stir the ingredients with ice and lemon peel for 15 seconds and strain into a chilled martini glass.

Glass Type: Chilled martini glass.

Garnish: Lemon twist or olive.

History: The Dry Martini is a classic cocktail known for its simplicity and elegance.

Curiosity: The choice between a lemon twist and an olive garnish is a matter of personal preference, and it can slightly alter the flavor profile of the drink.

.

DIRTY MARTINI

Recipe: 2 ½ oz Gin, 1/2 oz Dry Vermouth, 1/2 oz Olive Brine

Preparation: Stir the ingredients with ice for 15 seconds and strain into a chilled martini glass.

Glass Type: Chilled martini glass.

Garnish: Green olives or cocktail onions.

History: The Dirty Martini adds a savory and briny dimension to the classic Martini with the inclusion of olive brine.

Curiosity: The amount of olive brine can be adjusted to your taste, making the Martini dirtier or less so.

OLD FASHIONED

Recipe: 2 oz Bourbon, 1 Sugar Cube, Angostura and Orange Bitters.

Preparation: Stir the ingredients with ice with orange zest for 15 seconds and serve in a rock glass with a new orange zest.

Glass Type: Rock glass.

Garnish: Orange zest.

Ice Type: Large ice cube.

History: The Old Fashioned is one of the oldest known cocktails and is believed to have evolved in the early 19th century.

Curiosity: Muddling the sugar cube with bitters before adding the whiskey ensures an even distribution of flavor..

MANHATTAN

Recipe: 2 oz Rye Whiskey, 1 oz Sweet Vermouth, 2 dashes Angostura Bitters, 2 dashes Orange Bitter, 3 dashes of Peychaud's bitter

Preparation: Stir the ingredients with ice and strain into a chilled cocktail glass. Garnish with a Maraschino cherry.

Glass Type: Cocktail glass.

Garnish: Maraschino cherry.

History: The Manhattan cocktail is said to have been created in the 1870s at the Manhattan Club in New York City. It's a classic example of a stirred cocktail, and its elegant simplicity has made it a timeless favorite.

Curiosity: The original Manhattan recipe used rye whiskey, but bourbon is often used today, giving it a sweeter and smoother flavor profile.

BOULEVARDIER

Recipe: 1 ½ oz Bourbon, 1 oz Campari, 1 oz Sweet Vermouth.

Preparation: Stir the ingredients with ice and strain into a cocktail glass. Garnish with an orange twist.

Glass Type: Cocktail glass.

Garnish: Orange twist.

History: The Boulevardier is a classic cocktail that's essentially a Negroni with bourbon instead of gin. It was first documented in the 1927 book "Barflies and Cocktails" by Harry McElhone.

Curiosity: The name "Boulevardier" refers to a fashionable and worldly individual, and this cocktail is as sophisticated as its name implies.

SAZERAC

Recipe: 2 oz Rye Whiskey, 1 Sugar Cube, 2 dashes Peychaud's Bitters, Absinthe rinse.

Preparation: Rinse a chilled old-fashioned glass with absinthe, then discard the absinthe. In a separate glass, muddle the sugar cube and bitters. Add the rye whiskey and ice, stir, and strain into the prepared glass. Garnish with a lemon twist.

Glass Type: Old-fashioned glass.

Garnish: Lemon twist.

History: The Sazerac is a classic New Orleans cocktail, believed to be one of the world's oldest cocktails.

Curiosity: The Sazerac is often considered America's first cocktail.

DAIQUIRI

Recipe: 2 oz White Rum, 1 oz Fresh Lime Juice, 3/4 oz Simple Syrup.

Preparation: Shake the ingredients with ice and strain into a chilled cocktail glass.

Glass Type: Cocktail glass.

Garnish: Lime wheel or twist.

History: The Daiquiri is a simple and refreshing cocktail that originated in Cuba in the late 19th century. It gained worldwide popularity during the 20th century.

Curiosity: The most famous fan of the Daiquiri was Ernest Hemingway, who had his own variation called the "Hemingway Daiquiri," which included grapefruit and maraschino liqueur.

TOM COLLINS

Recipe: 2 oz Gin, 1 oz Fresh Lemon Juice, 1/2 oz Simple Syrup, Soda Water.

Preparation: Shake the gin, lemon juice, and simple syrup with ice, then strain into a tall glass filled with ice. Top with soda water, stir gently, and garnish with a lemon slice and cherry.

Glass Type: Collins glass.

Garnish: Lemon slice and cherry.

History: is a classic highball cocktail that dates back to the 19th century. It's believed to have originated in the United States and became especially popular during the cocktail renaissance of the 19th century.

SIDECAR

Recipe: 2 oz Cognac, 1 oz Triple Sec, 3/4 oz Fresh Lemon Juice.

Preparation: Shake the ingredients with ice and strain into a sugar-rimmed cocktail glass.

Glass Type: Cocktail glass.

Garnish: Lemon twist or wedge.

History: The Sidecar is believed to have been created during World War I, and it's a classic sour cocktail with a delightful balance of flavors.

Curiosity: The origin of the Sidecar is debated, with both London and Paris claiming to be its place of invention.

MARTINEZ

Recipe: 2 oz Old Tom Gin, 1 oz Sweet Vermouth, 0.25 oz Maraschino Liqueur, 2 dashes Angostura Bitters.

Preparation: Stir the ingredients with ice and strain into a chilled cocktail glass. Garnish with a lemon twist or cherry.

Glass Type: Cocktail glass.

Garnish: Lemon twist or cherry.

History: Often considered the precursor to the Martini and dates back to the mid-19th century.

Curiosity: Has seen various recipes and adaptations over the years, making its history fascinatingly complex. t was originally made with Old Tom gin, a sweeter style of gin.

BLOODY MARY

Recipe: 1 ½ oz Vodka, 3 oz Tomato Juice, 1/2 oz Fresh Lemon Juice, Various Spices and Seasonings (e.g., Worcestershire sauce, hot sauces, salt, pepper, and more).

Preparation: Build the ingredients in a shaker with ice, stir well, and strain into a highball glass filled with ice. Garnish with celery, olives, pickles, and a lemon wedge.

Glass Type: Highball glass.

Garnish: Assortment of items like celery, olives, pickles, lemon wedge.

History: The origins of the Bloody Mary are debated, but it's widely believed to have been created in the early 20th century. It has become a brunch and hangover cure favorite.

FRENCH 75

Recipe: 1 ½ oz Gin, 1/2 oz Fresh Lemon Juice, 1/2 oz Simple Syrup, Champagne.

Preparation: Shake the gin, lemon juice, and simple syrup with ice and strain into a chilled champagne flute. Top with Champagne.

Glass Type: Champagne flute.

Garnish: Lemon twist or cherry.

History: The French 75 is named after a World War I artillery piece and was first created in the early 20th century. It's known for its bubbly and refreshing character.

Curiosity: The French 75 is often considered a celebratory cocktail, perfect for toasting special occasions.

MOJITO

Recipe: 2 oz White Rum, 1 oz Fresh Lime Juice, 2 teaspoons Sugar, 6-8 Fresh Mint Leaves, Soda Water.

Preparation: Muddle the mint leaves and sugar in a glass. Add lime juice and rum, stir, and fill the glass with ice. Top with soda water and gently stir again.

Glass Type: Highball glass.

Garnish: Mint sprig and lime wheel.

History: The Mojito is a Cuban cocktail with roots dating back to the 16th century. It gained international fame as a favorite of Ernest Hemingway.

GIN FIZZ

Recipe: 2 oz Gin, 1 oz Fresh Lemon Juice, 3/4 oz Simple Syrup, Egg white Soda Water.

Preparation: Shake the gin, lemon juice, and simple syrup with ice, strain into a highball glass, and top with soda water.

Glass Type: Highball glass.

Garnish: Lemon wheel or twist.

History: The Gin Fizz is a classic cocktail with a history dating back to the 19th century. It's a member of the Fizz family, known for its effervescence.

Curiosity: The Gin Fizz has several variations, including the Ramos Gin Fizz, which is known for its elaborate preparation and frothy texture.

GIMLET

Recipe: 2 oz Gin, 0.75 oz Fresh Lime Juice, 0.5 oz Simple Syrup.

Preparation: Shake the ingredients with ice and strain into a chilled cocktail glass.

Glass Type: Cocktail glass.

Garnish: Lime wheel or twist.

History: The Gimlet is a simple yet classic cocktail that is believed to have been created in the early 20th century. It's known for its crisp and tangy flavor.

Curiosity: The Gimlet is often associated with the Royal Navy and was originally made with lime cordial to prevent scurvy..

MARGARITA

Recipe: 2 oz Tequila, 1 oz Triple Sec, 3/4 oz Fresh Lime Juice, Salt (for rimming the glass).

Preparation: Rim the edge of the glass with salt. Shake the tequila, triple sec, and lime juice with ice, then strain into the prepared glass.

Glass Type: Margarita glass.

Garnish: Lime wheel or wedge.

History: The Margarita's origin is debated, but it's widely associated with Mexico and has been a popular cocktail since the mid-20th century.

Curiosity: There are numerous variations of the Margarita, including the frozen Margarita and the spicy Jalapeño Margarita.

HIGH BALL

Recipe: 2 oz Whiskey (or preferred spirit), 4-6 oz Soda Water, Ice, Garnish (e.g., lemon or lime wedge, cherry, or mint sprig).

Preparation: Fill a highball glass with ice. Add whiskey, top with soda water, and gently stir.

Glass Type: Highball glass (Collins glass).

Garnish: Lemon or lime wedge, cherry, or mint sprig.

History: A classic cocktail dating back to the late 19th century.

Cultural Note: In Japan, the Highball has gained significant popularity and is often celebrated for its simplicity and the art of creating a perfect balance between whisky and soda, reflecting Japanese precision and craftsmanship.

CONTEMPORARY CLASSICS

The contemporary classic cocktail family represents a fusion of innovation and tradition, capturing the spirit of modern mixology while paying homage to the time-honored cocktail culture. These drinks are characterized by their touch of creativity, a testament to the evolving world of cocktails

THE PISCO SOUR

Recipe: 1 ½ oz Pisco, 1/2 oz Cointreau, 1 oz Lime Juice, 3/4 oz Sugar Syrup, Egg white

Preparation: Dry shake, then ice shake, and strain into a chilled coupe martini glass.

Glass Type: Chilled coupe martini glass.

Garnish: Orange zest and three dashes of Angostura.

History: The Pisco Sour is the national drink of both Peru and Chile, with origins dating back to the early 20th century.

Curiosity: The dry shake followed by an ice shake ensures a frothy, velvety texture in the Pisco Sour.

COSMOPOLITAN

Recipe: 1 ½ oz Citron Vodka, 1/2 oz Cointreau, 1 oz Lime Juice, 1 ½ oz Cranberry Juice.

Preparation: Shake and strain into a chilled martini glass.

Glass Type: Chilled martini glass.

Garnish: Orange zest.

Ice Type: None.

History: The Cosmopolitan gained widespread popularity in the 1990s, partly due to its appearance on the TV show "Sex and the City."

Curiosity: A quality triple sec and fresh lime juice are essential for a well-balanced Cosmopolitan.

Mixology Tip: Try a cranberry juice reduction to intensify the cranberry flavor without diluting the drink.

TOMMY'S MARGARITA

Recipe: 1 ½ oz Tequila Reposado, 1/2 oz Triple Sec, 1 oz Lime Juice, ½ oz Agave.

Preparation: Shake & strain, serve in a rock glass with ice.

Glass Type: Rock glass.

Garnish: Dried lime wheel.

Ice Type: Cubed ice.

History: This Margarita variation comes from Tommy's Mexican Restaurant in San Francisco, renowned for its tequila selection.

Curiosity: Using 100% agave tequila and agave nectar instead of triple sec creates a more agave-forward, agave-sweetened Margarita.

Mixology Tip: Enhance the presentation by rimming the glass with a blend of salt and chili powder for a spicy kick.

PALOMA

Recipe: 1 ½ oz Tequila Reposado, 1 oz Lime, ½ oz Agave, 2 oz Grapefruit, Splash of soda

Preparation: Shake & strain, serve in a rock glass with ice.

Glass Type: Rock glass.

Garnish: Grapefruit zest.

Ice Type: Cubed ice.

History: The Paloma is a classic Mexican cocktail, beloved for its simplicity and refreshing taste.

Curiosity: Use fresh grapefruit juice for the best flavor in a Paloma.

Mixology Tip: For an extra twist, add a hint of smoked salt to the rim for a smoky-sweet contrast.

WHISKEY SMASH

Recipe: 2 oz Whiskey, 1 oz Lime Juice, ¾ oz Syrup, 4 Mint Leaves.

Preparation: Shake and strain with mint, serve in a rock glass with ice.

Glass Type: Rock glass.

Garnish: Mint and a lemon twist.

Ice Type: Crushed ice.

History: The Whiskey Smash is a classic cocktail with a history dating back to the 19th century.

Curiosity: Slapping the mint leaves before using them can release more of their essential oils and enhance the aroma of the cocktail.

LYCHEE MARTINI

Recipe: 1 ½ oz Vodka, ½ oz X-Rated or Passion fruit liqueur, 1 ½ oz Lychee Juice, 1 oz Lime, 1/4 oz Simple Syrup.

Preparation: Shake and strain, serve in a chilled martini glass.

Glass Type: Chilled martini glass.

Garnish: Lychee on a bamboo stick.

Ice Type: None.

History: The Lychee Martini is a modern classic, showcasing the sweet and delicate flavor of lychee.

Curiosity: Ensure that the lychee juice is fresh and not too sweet to maintain a balanced flavor.

DESSERT COCKTAILS

Dessert cocktails offer a delightful conclusion to a meal or a sweet treat on their own. These concoctions bring together the rich and sweet flavors of various liqueurs, creams, and decadent ingredients to create a liquid dessert experience. From classic favorites to inventive twists, dessert cocktails are the perfect way to satisfy your sweet tooth and end a meal on a high note.

ESPRESSO MARTINI

Name: Espresso Martini

Recipe: 1 ½ oz Vanilla Vodka, ½ oz Tia Maria, 1 Espresso.

Preparation: Hard shake and fine strain, serve in a chilled martini glass.

Glass Type: Chilled martini glass.

Garnish: Three coffee beans.

History: The Espresso Martini is a delightful coffee-flavored cocktail that has gained popularity in recent decades.

Curiosity: The three coffee beans garnish is said to represent health, happiness, and prosperity.

ESPRESSO MARGARITA

Recipe: 1 ½ oz Tequila Reposada, 1/2 oz Tia Marina, 1 Espresso.

Preparation: Hard shake and fine strain, serve in a chilled martini coupe glass.

Glass Type: Chilled martini coupe glass.

Garnish: Three coffee beans and a line of coffee.

Ice Type: None.

History: The XO Espresso Martini adds a touch of tequila to the classic Espresso Martini.

Curiosity: The line of coffee on top of the cocktail enhances the coffee aroma and flavor.

CARIBBEAN ESPRESSO MARTINI

Recipe: 1 ½ oz Spiced Rum, ½ Kaluha, 1 Espresso.

Preparation: Hard shake and fine strain, serve in a chilled martini coupe glass.

Glass Type: Chilled martini coupe glass.

Garnish: Three coffee beans and a dehydrated pineapple.

Ice Type: None.

History: The Caribbean Espresso Martini using Caribbean spiced rum to the classic Espresso Martini.

Curiosity: The dehydrated pineapple on top of the cocktail enhances the coffee and rum aroma and flavor.

CHOCOALMOND

Recipe: ½ Chocolate Liqueur, ½ Almond Liqueur, 1 oz Vodka, 1 ½ Milk.

Preparation: Shake and strain in a martini glass.

Glass Type: Martini glass.

Garnish: Chocolate chips.

Ice Type: None.

Mixology Tip: The addition of milk gives the Chocoalmond a creamy and rich texture, garnish with grated nutmeg or a dusting of cocoa powder to enhance the aroma.

TIRAMISU MARTINI

Recipe: 1 oz Vanilla Vodka, 1 oz Kahlúa, 1 oz Cream, 1 oz Espresso.

Preparation: Shake with ice and strain into a chilled martini glass.

Glass Type: Chilled martini glass.

Garnish: Sprinkle of cocoa powder.

Ice Type: None.

History: Inspired by the classic Italian dessert, the Tiramisu Martini combines the flavors of coffee, cream, and cocoa.

AMARETTO SOUR

Recipe: 1 1/2 oz Amaretto, 1/2 oz Triple Sec, 1 oz fresh lime, 1/2 oz simple syrup

Preparation: Shake with ice and strain into a rock glass with sugar rim, garnish

Glass Type: Rock Glass

Garnish: Orange peel and cherry

Ice Type: Rocks

History: classic drink made with amaretto liqueur, lemon juice, and simple syrup. Its origins date back to the mid-20th century, and it's known for its sweet and slightly tart flavor with a hint of almond.

MOCKTAILS

Mocktails, short for "mock cocktails," are non-alcoholic beverages designed to deliver all the flavor and fun of traditional cocktails without the alcohol. These refreshing and creative concoctions are perfect for those seeking a delightful alternative. Mocktails combine a colorful array of ingredients, from fresh fruits to herbs and sparkling water, to offer a wide range of flavors and experiences.

SHIRLEY TEMPLE

Ingredients: Ginger Ale or Lemon-Lime Soda, Orange Juice, Grenadine Syrup

Preparation: Fill a glass with ice, pour the ginger ale or lemon-lime soda over the ice., add the orange juice into the glass. Slowly pour the grenadine syrup down the side of the glass, allowing it to sink to the bottom.

Garnish: Maraschino cherries

History: The Shirley Temple, named after the famous child actress Shirley Temple, was created in the 1930s. This delightful non-alcoholic drink gained popularity for its sweet and fizzy taste, making it a favorite among kids and adults alike.

WHAT A TIKI!

Ingredients: Pineapple, Passion Fruit, Strawberry, Coconut.

Preparation: Prepare a mocktail by blending these ingredients.

Glass Type: Tiki glass.

Garnish: A pineapple slice, a passion fruit half, and a seasonal fruit

Ice Type: Crushed ice.

Curiosity: Tiki-inspired mocktails are known for their tropical and fruity flavors. The garnish enhances the visual appeal and tropical feel of this mocktail.

MOKHITO

Ingredients: Lime, Sugar Syrup, Mint Leaf, Ginger Ale.

Preparation: Prepare a mocktail by mixing these ingredients.

Glass Type: Highball glass.

Garnish: Mint sprig, lime wheel, and a paper straw.

Ice Type: Cubed ice.

Curiosity: Mokhito is a non-alcoholic take on the classic Mojito. The combination of fresh lime and mint gives the Mokhito a refreshing and zesty taste.

Mixology Tip: Slightly muddle the mint leaves in the glass before adding the other ingredients to release their flavor. Add any fresh fruit to make it more delicious.

CHILL IN LONG BAY

Ingredients: Orange Juice, Pineapple Juice, Mango, Grenadine.

Preparation: Prepare a mocktail by mixing these ingredients.

Glass Type: Hurricane glass.

Garnish: Orange wheel, pineapple and mint.

Ice Type: Crushed ice.

Curiosity: Mocktails like Chill in Long Bay often emulate the flavors of tropical cocktails. The name comes from a famous beach in Turks and Caicos. The layering of ingredients creates a visually appealing and vibrant mocktail.

RASP-LEMONADE

Ingredients: Lemon Juice, Raspberry Syrup, Soda Water.

Preparation: Mix lemon juice and raspberry syrup, add ice, and top with soda water.

Glass Type: Highball glass.

Garnish: Fresh raspberries and a lemon slice.

Ice Type: Cubed ice.

Curiosity: A vibrant and fruity mocktail that combines the tartness of lemon with the sweetness of raspberries.

CUCUMBER BASIL SPARKLER

Ingredients: Fresh Cucumber, Basil Leaves, Lime Juice, Simple Syrup, Soda Water.

Preparation: Muddle cucumber and basil with lime juice and simple syrup, add ice, and top with soda water.

Garnish: Cucumber wheel and basil sprig.

History: This modern mocktail combines the cool and refreshing notes of cucumber with the herbal infusion of basil.

Keep in mind that each cocktail is an opportunity to surprise and delight, creating unforgettable memories for anyone privileged to taste your creations. Your journey into mixology has only just begun, and as you explore new recipes and experiment with ingredients, always carry with you the passion and curiosity that make each cocktail a work of art.

With your new knowledge base, you are ready to lift your shaker, shake, stir, and craft extraordinary cocktails. Whether you are a seasoned bartender or an aspiring mixologist, keep and use this handbook as your guide to creating unforgettable experiences through the magical world of cocktails.

Made in the USA
Columbia, SC
02 May 2025

57186052R00102